Rebels and Royals

20 Stories from British History

Geraldine McCaughrean was born in North London and has a degree in Education. She has been writing full time for many years and has won the Whitbread Award, the Guardian Children's Fiction Award, the Carnegie Medal and, most recently, the Blue Peter Book of the Year Award.

Rebels and Royals is the second in a series of five books which will include all 100 stories from *Britannia: 100 Great Stories from British History*.

Rebels and Royals

20 Stories from British History

Geraldine McCaughrean

Illustrated by Richard Brassey

Dolphin Paperbacks

For Rachel

This edition first published in Great Britain in 2001
by Orion Children's Books
a division of the Orion Publishing Group Ltd
Orion House
5 Upper St Martin's Lane
London   WC2H 9EA

The stories in this volume were originally published
as part of *Britannia: 100 Great Stories from British History*,
first published by Orion Children's Books in 1999.

A catalogue record for this book is available
from the British Library

Printed in Great Britain by
The Guernsey Press Co. Ltd, Guernsey, C. I.

ISBN   1 85881 852 4

Contents

Introduction   vii

Canute Defies the Sea   1

"Macbeth Does Murder Sleep"   5

Lady Godiva's Shameless Ride   10

Swearing on the Bones   17

Hereward the Wake   24

Margaret's Prayer   31

Who Killed Red Rufus?   37

The White Ship   42

"This Turbulent Priest"   48

Fair Rosamond   57

The Troubadour Rescues His King   62

The Three Outlaws   69

Cuckoos   77

Lost in the Wash   82

"Wrap Me Up in a Cloak of Gold"   87

"A Prince Who Speaks No Word of English"   92

Robert the Bruce and the Spider   98

The Brawling Scottish Wench   105

The Black Prince Wins His Spurs   110

"Oss! Oss!" "Wee Oss!"   116

Introduction

During the first millennium, Britain was a battleground for a succession of settlers and invaders. When the Normans finally came in 1066, they were resented as much as any of the previous 'incomers'. It was the Saxon hatred of Normans which gave rise to the legends – mostly invented – of brave resistance fighters; Hereward the Wake, Robin Hood, Clym of the Cleugh – and to folktales about 'wicked King John' and 'devilish Rufus'. Then, of course, there were the Norman counter-stories justifying their conquest . . .

Meanwhile, Wales and Scotland, largely unconquered and fiercely independent, got on with their own power struggles and myth-making.

Watch out, as you read, for efforts to sway your sympathies towards one cause or another. What you will be seeing is the reason these stories came into being.

Canute Defies the Sea

about 1020

Good or bad, a king draws flatterers like a horse draws flies, and King Canute, in his fenland kingdom, had accumulated a veritable swarm.

"The sun is shining today, my lord, because it is glad to see you so well!"

"The kings of all Europe are trembling this morning, your honour, at the thought of your might and wisdom!"

"The Pope himself is surely envious of your saintliness, my lord!"

Canute stood up suddenly. "I dare say I could cross swords with the moon and win," he suggested.

"Oh, no doubt! No question, my lord King!"

"And command the sea itself to do my bidding."

"The seas, my lord King, would be honoured to serve you," said the toadies.

"Then take hold of my throne – you – you – and you! – and be so good as to carry it down to the beach," said Canute, to the court's surprise.

The sea lay vast and grey, breathing shallowly, lapping at shells on the wet sand. Canute had his throne placed a few steps from the water's edge and sat in it. His courtiers stood about, hands clasped on their stomachs, smiles set hard. The tide was rising.

"Hold off, Sea!" commanded Canute, holding

up one royal hand. "I, Canute, say you shall not rise today!" His courtiers looked at each other, but went on smiling. "Stay back, thou great wet thing!" commanded Canute, holding up both royal hands. "I, Canute, command it!"

But, of course, the sea continued to lap the shore, and every seventh wave ran higher up the beach, wetting dry sand, turning dry stones. Soon the legs of the throne were awash. The royal feet were distinctly wet. The courtiers, hopping about dismally, kept on smiling.

"O unruly and uppish monster! Do you defy me? Do you dare to invade my kingdom?" protested Canute. A large grey wave wetted everyone to the knees and the backwash dragged sand from under their sodden velvet shoes.

"I really think, your Majesty," began the chancellor, "it's not quite safe to . . ."

"But you told me I was more powerful than the sea!" Canute retorted, and he sat fast, until the throne itself was being rocked by large cold waves, and his courtiers were up to their waists in brine.

"Scurvy ocean!" Canute declaimed. "I see that you have not heard of King Canute the All-Powerful! I see we must wrestle hand-to-hand!"

"No! No, my lord!" cried several of his courtiers, wading through the swell. "Please!"

"You mean to say I am *not* all-powerful?" said Canute with exaggerated amazement. "You mean to say that the winds and waves do *not* obey God's anointed king?"

"I –"

"We –"

"Ah –"

"No? Then in future, I'll thank you *not* to tell me such monumental untruths, gentlemen. I look to you for your help and advice and measured opinions. I do not look to you for flattery, lies and servility. Do I make myself clear?"

"Perfectly!" howled the court in unison as a great wave broke and left them flailing ashore, tripping and gasping, and dipping for their hats in the unheeding sea.

At one time, King Canute ruled three kingdoms – England, Norway and Denmark – and spent long periods overseas. But his twenty-year rule in England was a time of relative stability. After his death, his empire fell apart as his sons fought for supremacy. His first heir died. His second heir, Hardaknut, was hated, unlike Knut who was revered as a wise, religious man.

The story of Knut and the sea was and is frequently mis-told, as if Canute believes the sea will obey him, but only because listeners like to hear of the proud being humbled.

"Macbeth Does Murder Sleep"

1040
(Shakespeare, Macbeth)

Macbeth was exultant as he rode homeward from the coast. He had fought a whole fleet of Danish invaders and won. At his side rode his friend Banquo, Thane of Lochaber. Suddenly, out of the dank, wreathing mist, three old women appeared. "Hail Macbeth, Thane of Glamis. Hail Macbeth, Thane of Cawdor. All hail Macbeth, soon to be King of Scotland!"

"None of these titles is mine," said Macbeth. "You mistake me for my father even to call me Thane of Glamis." But perhaps these old crones were witches. Perhaps they were blessed with the magic powers and could see events in the future as other people saw fish in a pond.

"Have you nothing to say to me?" asked Banquo, eager for a prophecy of his own.

"No king thou, but a father of kings!" chanted the gnarled, weather-blasted crones. Then they were gone, swallowed up by the mist . . . and approaching, each from a different direction, were two messengers. Macbeth's father was dead: the title "Thane of Glamis" had passed to him. And King Duncan, in acknowledgement of his victory over the Danes, had awarded valiant Macbeth the estates of Cawdor.

Two prophecies come true in as many minutes! The news shook Macbeth more than any battle. For if two prophecies could come true, why not the third? Might Macbeth one day be king? The thought warmed him like a great dog leaning against his belly.

If Macbeth were ambitious, his wife Gruoch was eaten up with ambition. There was royal blood in her veins and it cried out for power. When she heard tell of the three witches, heard of her husband's new titles and saw the hunger in him to be king, she swept aside all his qualms, drowned out the whispers of his conscience, telling him, "Yes! Murder Duncan and be king!"

Duncan and his son, Prince Malcolm, were invited to stay at the castle of the Macbeths, near Inverness. After the old man had gone to bed, Gruoch drugged his

6

bodyguards and, when they were slumped snoring by the King's bed, Macbeth took their daggers and stabbed Duncan through the heart. In the morning, when the body was found, he feigned horror and outrage – and, blaming the guards, killed them outright.

Duncan's son, Malcolm, was not fooled for one moment. He fled – over the border into England, rightly supposing that he was the only person who stood between Macbeth and the crown which he and Gruoch so insanely craved.

The great prize was won, just as the witches had said it would be. The metal crown weighed heavy on his temples . . . but the second prophecy dragged like a sea-anchor on his heart. Banquo's sons would be kings? How? Why not Macbeth's?

He would kill Banquo. No! He would pay for Banquo to be killed: a king does not need to sully his hands. It was done: another obstacle removed, another bloody notch cut in Macbeth's conscience.

But he could not rest easy until he had visited the three old hags again.

He was not disappointed; the three old women were still there on the heath. Their mumbling toothless heads emerged from the rocky dark like tortoises emerging from their shells. "Show me the future!" he demanded. "Is my crown secure? Am I safe from my enemies?"

They looked at him with eyes as yellow as cesspits. "Macbeth shall not be conquered till Birnam Wood comes to Dunsinane."

Macbeth gave a shrill, gasping laugh. Safe, then! Birnam Wood stood several miles from his castle at Dunsinane, and how could a *forest* move? He told his wife. He told his men-at-arms: "I am invincible.

Nothing can defeat me till Birnam Wood comes to Dunsinane!"

Meanwhile, in England, Malcolm threw himself on the mercy of Edward the Confessor and scuffed his heels around the English court. He won over to his cause the Earl of Northumberland and a thane called Macduff, wronged and driven out of Scotland by King Macbeth. They raised an army and marched on Dunsinane: Macbeth's spies quickly brought him word of it, but Macbeth only laughed. Cloaked round in his magical prophecy, he was smugly complacent.

A servant came stumbling into the room, eyes bulging, mouth a-jabber. "The wood, sire! The wood . . . !" He almost died, Macbeth's fingers around his throat, for the news he brought: that Dunsinane Wood appeared to be *moving towards the castle*.

Macbeth flung him aside and ran to the battlements. The raw wind stung his eyes to tears as he stared. The prophecy clamoured in his head, indistinguishable from the alarm bell.

In marching through Birnam Wood, Macduff had told every soldier to strip a branch from the trees and to carry it, and so mask the size and nature of the force coming against Macbeth. It would keep him guessing.

But as far as Macbeth was concerned, the battle was already lost. His heart crumpled within him. He looked around and saw that his men, too, remembered the prophecy. It hamstrung them; it set their sword-hands shaking. With one last effort of will, he rallied them to the attack. The portcullis lifted, and they forayed out to meet the enemy they knew would destroy them . . .

The source of this story is Raphael Holinshed's *Chronicles* of 1577, and it was this book which Shakespeare would have used when he wrote his tragedy, *Macbeth*. It is known that Macbeth seized the throne by murdering Duncan, and that he suffered defeat at the hands of Prince Malcolm. But Holinshed made free with the facts and Shakespeare adjusted them even more.

In fact Macbeth ruled Scotland for seventeen years, and his reign was thought of as a time of prosperity. He gave large sums to charity (possibly to salve a bad conscience) and went on pilgrimage to Rome. And although he lost the battle at Dunsinane, he escaped and survived three further years before he was killed by Malcolm. Shakespeare depicted Lady Macbeth as a woman driven to madness then suicide by her guilt, but Gruoch's true fate is unknown. She simply disappeared.

In the context of eleventh-century Scotland, there is nothing remarkable about the violence of Macbeth's rise and fall. It was the masterpiece Shakespeare wove around the events which immortalized this obscure chapter of Scottish history.

Lady Godiva's Shameless Ride

about 1050

People did not know how Godiva could bear to live with Leofric: his meanness, his little acts of spite, his nasty temper. And she so kind and beautiful! People said what a shame it was that the best wives sometimes marry the worst men.

But Lady Godiva loved her husband. Even though he was not handsome or gentle or even very pleasant, she genuinely loved him. It saddened her that he was so unpopular with the people. Leofric was Earl of Chester, which gave him, for his income, the revenue of the city of Coventry. Tithes, rent, fines, fees and levies, Leofric took them all. If anyone could not pay, he evicted them. Sometimes Lady Godiva would try to help the hardest pressed, with a coin from her own purse, but she had to do it in secret: Leofric looked on charity as throwing good money after bad.

"The Bible tells us we should help the poor," Godiva pointed out gently.

"The Bible tells us to work hard and pay our taxes," said Leofric disagreeably. "They have plenty of money, you take my word. You shouldn't believe their hard-luck stories."

He raised the taxes, until the people complained aloud. Then he punished them with higher taxes.

"Don't do this, husband," said Lady Godiva one

day, as he sat composing a new proclamation. "I have never contradicted you before, but this new tax of yours is wrong. It will cause such suffering."

"Keep your place, woman," snapped Leofric. "What do you know of such things?"

"But the people will hate you for this tax. Don't do it, I beg you."

Leofric laughed. "What do I care if they hate me, so long as they pay?"

Lady Godiva breathed deeply. "If you really need this money, I will give it you out of my own inheritance."

That silenced his laughing. "I'll have you know, madam, that your money is already mine to do with as I please. And I do not please to use my *own money* to pay what the people of Coventry owe me."

Lady Godiva was quiet for so long that Leofric thought he had won the argument. But then his wife drew herself up to her full height. "My money may be yours, Leofric, but I think you will agree, my body is my own. If you will not be ashamed, I must be ashamed for you. Withdraw this latest tax . . . or I shall ride naked through the streets of Coventry in token of the people you have left naked to wind and rain."

Leofric snorted with scorn. "*You*? The virtuous Lady Godiva? You would die of shame, and I would die of laughing." His quill nib scratched on the parchment like a rat on a granary wall.

Next Sunday, in every church in Coventry, there was an astonishing announcement made. "Tomorrow, Lady Godiva, wife of the Earl of Chester, will ride naked through the streets of the city. Let her shame fall on Leofric for his greed."

Some priests whispered it, some choked on the word "naked", some never even reached the end before uproar broke out. Soon everyone had grasped the news, including Leofric, dozing sleepily in his scarlet padded pew.

His first thought was to put his wife under lock and key, but Godiva was too quick for him; she had already gone into hiding. "She will never do it," he comforted himself, but he did not sleep well that night, in his big Coventry house.

Next morning, he woke to the sound of hooves on the cobbles below. They rang through the silent city streets. He threw open the shutters and shouted along

the whole length of Broadgate: "Don't do this, Godiva! Don't do this to me!"

The rising sun shone on her long, loose hair falling over her bare shoulders, breaking over the horse's rump. She rode bareback, astride her grey mare. From the crown of her head to the soles of her feet, she was stark naked.

Godiva did not feel the cold; her skin burned with shame and anger. This was not the act of some brazen woman carrying out a shocking dare. Godiva was humiliating herself in the hope of humbling her husband. She did not round her shoulders nor cower down over the horse's neck, but inwardly she knew

what agonies she would suffer when exposed to the whistles and stares of a market-day crowd.

Was this not a market day?

On market days, the city was busy even before sun-up, crowded with people setting up stalls, opening the front windows of their houses to trade with passers-by; countryfolk walking in from the outlying villages with eggs, vegetables and wickerwork. On market days carts vied for right of way; tinkers bawled and shouted.

So was this *not* a market day?

The streets were so quiet! No carts rattled over the cobbles. No one was setting up their wares in the market place. Godiva raised her eyes. Every house shutter was closed, every door shut. Somewhere a dog barked. Water gurgled down the drain in the middle of the road. But no one shouted, no one pushed a handcart through the alleyways. No one stared.

Leofric came running, Godiva's cloak bundled up in his arms. He tried to throw it over her, but she shrugged it off and it fell into the drain. "Godiva, please! Look at you! You'll die of cold. I'll die of shame! What are you doing to me?"

"You have stripped the people bare with your taxes and your levies," said Godiva looking steadfastly ahead. "The people of Coventry will think no less of me for this. But *your* name will go down in history as the man who swindled Coventry." Her bare heels thudded into the horse's withers, and it broke into a trot.

Leofric looked around him, cringing, anticipating the laughter, the hoots, the crude jokes that would shower down on his lovely wife and on him. These people were nothing but despicable peasants, after all.

He saw the closed windows, the shut doors, the empty alleyways and the silent market place. Every citizen had turned his face to the wall and shut his eyes, sooner than shame Lady Godiva.

Not quite *every* one shut their eyes. Tom Henny rubbed his sweaty hands in glee and knelt down by the keyhole. Tom often went out late at night and peeped through shutters in the hope of seeing a pretty girl undressing. The sight of Lady Godiva naked was going to be sweet as honey! Let the other prudes shut their eyes: Tom would look his fill. He licked his lips as the clip-clop of hooves came closer. He pressed his eye to the keyhole . . .

A sudden unseasonable swirl of wind gusted down the street, lifting an eddy of dust. Tom Henny gave a scream of pain. A piece of grit had embedded itself in his eye. As the hooves clopped by outside, he had no thought of seeing Lady Godiva, dressed or naked. All he could think about was getting the grit out of his eye.

Leofric waited in Cathedral Square for his wife to ride back the way she had gone. "I give in!" he called, as she came into view. He spoke in a loud voice, knowing the town stood listening behind its closed shutters. "You have your wish! I shall not impose the new tax. If that earns me the respect of these decent people, I shall be rich enough."

The town remembered that day – wrote of it in the annals of the county, with a sigh of admiration for Lady Godiva. They saved their scorn for Tom Henny – Peeping Tom, as they called him. He had to endure the silent contempt of his neighbours as, collar up, hat pulled down, he went about, day by lonely day, trying to conceal his one blind eye.

15

The story of Lady Godiva's ride through Coventry was first written down by Roger of Wendover, two centuries after the supposed event. The character of Peeping Tom was added later still. But Lady Godiva undoubtedly was the generous benefactor suggested by the story. She endowed monasteries at Stow and Coventry. Until recently she was referred to as mother of Hereward the Wake (see page 30), though there are no historical grounds to think she was. She outlived her husband by twenty-three years and died in 1080.

Swearing on the Bones
1064

Before the death of Edward the Confessor, promises were flying about more plentiful than starlings around the spires of Westminster Abbey. King Edward favoured Harold, Earl of Wessex, as his successor, but William, Duke of Normandy, had a powerful claim as well. There was bound to be a struggle for power when the old King died. Already the rival candidates were trying to extract promises of support from anyone and everyone.

Then Harold was shipwrecked on the shores of France, and taken prisoner. Duke William was informed, and arranged for Harold to be set free. Indeed, Harold was very glad to escape a stone dungeon floor and sharing his food with rats.

So when the two men met, there was no un-pleasantness between them. Harold said how grateful he was. William said it was nothing: all that he asked in exchange was that Harold should swear to forfeit his claim and help William to his rightful place on the throne of England. "Here. Your word on it!"

The table was spread with cloth of gold. Wine stains and fragments of chicken speckled it, but William cleared space to set down the Gospels.

Did Harold wet his lips or look shiftily about? Did he hide one hand under his tabard and cross his

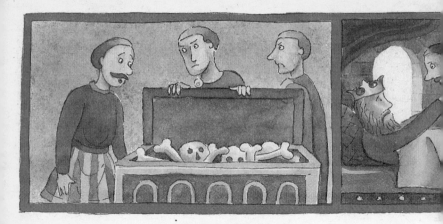

fingers? No. Harold had lied to better men than this before now. He would lie with gusto, knowing that the throne rightfully belonged to him, knowing that God would turn a deaf ear. Solemnly, he laid his hand on the Gospels – William covered it with his own, sword-hardened palm and Harold swore: "to help William, Duke of Normandy, to win the crown of England". The hand lifted off his. He felt his freedom already. He could not wait to get back across the Channel. With the flourish of a magician, William of Normandy drew off the cloth of gold; it cracked like a banner on a windy day. His eyes were still on Harold, still fixing him, as a cat fixes a cornered mouse. Two armed men sprang forward, and Harold thought, they are going to stab me.

But the two soldiers only lifted the table top off its trestle legs to reveal, underneath, a big carved, darkwood chest. That too was opened. Inside it lay something which stood Harold's hair on end.

"Bones?" he said.

"The relics of a dozen saints," said William. "Can

there be any oath so solemn as the oath sworn on the relics of a saint?"

Harold went pale and shuddered. Not for an instant did he consider keeping his promise, laying aside his claim to the throne. But it was as if, in that moment, the windows of heaven closed and the angels deserted him.

Edward the Confessor did name Harold his heir; the Witan Council of wise men elected him, too, and Harold said nothing in defence of Duke William's claim. In short, he broke his promise, in order to be crowned King of England.

William wrote reminding Harold "of the oath which thou hast sworn with thy hand upon good and holy relics". But Harold wrote back that he had promised what did not belong to him, "a promise which I could not in any way perform". War was just a matter of time.

That year Halley's comet swung low through the sky like a burning tear. What could it mean? Did it foretell disaster?

William mustered his invasion forces, but for a long time the wind blew against him. Indeed, hurricanes smashed his ships and drowned his crews. Perhaps the saints were not on his side after all. Overhead the comet hurtled on through space, bearing the colours of neither side, instead unfurling a blank white banner.

Then the Norwegian King invaded England from the north. Harold had to hurry north to Stamford Bridge and counter the invasion. He fought a masterly battle – defeated the Norwegians, and rode south again, flushed with victory. Perhaps the comet plunging past the earth meant disaster for the Northmen, after all. Or perhaps it acclaimed the coming of Harold the Victor, a king destined to win many such victories.

His fleet was still sailing up and down the Channel, guarding the south coast against William's threatened invasion. Still an adverse wind kept William from setting sail. Harold, rushing south as fast as his battle-weary army could go, smiled every time he saw a weathercock on a church roof.

But then the English navy ran out of provisions and had to put back to port for more. *That* was when the wind came about, when William set sail. Four days after the battle of Stamford Bridge, William of Normandy landed his invasion force at Pevensey Bay.

First ashore were the archers, shaven-headed, in short tunics. Then came the horsemen, in coats of mail, with polished conical helmets, lances and heavy broadswords. Next came the workmen: sappers and armourers, smiths and fletchers. And last of all came William himself.

Tripping, he promptly pitched on his face in the sand

and cut himself. Superstitious dread seized on a thousand men. Was this an omen? Had the comet in the sky signalled disaster for the Normans and not, after all, for Harold the Oath-breaker?

With remarkable presence of mind (considering the pain in his knees), Duke William closed his fist around a lump of sandy soil and held it aloft. "Now I have taken possession of England and will defend it with my blood!" he bellowed, and a thousand men let go their pent-up breath in a gasp of relief.

Harold was in no mood to negotiate. Besides, he had already parcelled out England to his own choice of friends, knights and barons: they would never let him abdicate. So the English troops, only returned in the nick of time and exhausted from the high-speed journey, made their stand near Hastings, mustered on top of a hill, behind a wooden palisade. It gave the Normans marshy ground to cover and a steep climb before they could even cross swords with the English.

With horrid fascination the English watched a single rider break ranks and ride forward up the hill: a troubadour-knight known as Taillefer or "the Iron Cleaver". He began to sing – a ballad of heroism and self-sacrifice – and as he sang, he tossed his sword in the air and caught it, again and again, so that its arcing, somersaulting blade sliced the sunlight into spinning shards. It mesmerized the eye – such juggling, such foolhardy panache. With suicidal daring, Taillefer hurled himself on the first two Englishmen in his path, and cut them down, before he himself was pulled down and lost from sight amid the confusion of the first charge.

The Normans were galvanized into action. Time and

again they made sallies up the hill, shouting, "God strengthen us!" but were thwarted by the wooden palisade and javelins thrown back with the cry, "God Almighty!" Duke William, leading a charge uphill, felt the horse under him shudder then plunge to its knees, a spear in its chest. But he no sooner hit the ground than he was on his feet again, leading the assault on the palisade. They captured the hill, but not the English standard. That stood at King Harold's side, surrounded by his finest knights, and evening was coming on.

"Shoot your arrows into the sky!" called William to his archers. "Let them fall on the English faces!"

The archers arched their backs, squinted into the evening clouds. They fired their arrows upwards as if they would shoot the very evening star out of the sky. And their arrows fell like rain.

Harold looked up at the sound of whistling in the skies, and saw a hail of death falling on him. It was the last thing he saw. An arrow entered his eye, filled his brain with light and then with darkness. Like a comet plummeting away into unfathomable space, Harold fell: from noise to silence, from glory to oblivion. All around him the English still cried, with futile desperation, "God Almighty!"

But all Harold could hear was the rattling of bones underground.

The full story of Harold's sworn oath, the Norman invasion and the battle of Hastings is told in the Bayeux Tapestry, a long strip of linen embroidered in wool, probably by English needlewomen. The embroidery was commissioned by Bishop Odo, half-brother of William the Conqueror, to commemorate the victory. It naturally presents William in a good light and Harold as an oathbreaker who deserved to lose the crown. The comet is there, foretelling Harold's downfall.

Unfortunately, it is now thought that the figure seen pulling an arrow from his eye may not be Harold at all. So the best "known" fact about Harold (i.e. that he died of an arrow in the eye) may not even be true. No other record exists describing his death.

Hereward the Wake

1070

He was always a wild boy. From the start, Hereward was so wild that they say his own father declared him an outlaw and drove him out to live in the forests and fens. Hereward was a young man full of rage and fire. But when the Normans came and the country was taken out of Saxon hands, Hereward's rage suddenly found a fitting target. He vowed to drive the Normans out of England or make them wish they had never come.

The good Saxon abbot of St Peter's Abbey had been replaced with a Norman one. So Hereward felt free to storm the Abbey and pillage it of every candlestick and cross and chalice. A military campaign needs funds, after all.

But afterwards, a dream rose into Hereward's sleep like mist rising off the fens. He saw St Peter, angry and woebegone, searching, searching under every bush and in the hollow of every tree. He was searching for his treasure. "Oh Hereward, Hereward, what have I ever done to you?" glared the eyes of St Peter.

At first light, Hereward packed up the treasure of St Peter's Abbey and sent it back – every last chalice, plate and candlestick. "My quarrel is with the Normans, not with the saints," he told his bewildered men.

Armed with his sword Brainbiter, Hereward the

Wakeful harried the Normans as a fox harries a chicken coop. Suddenly, stealthily, out of darkness or mist, his band of loyal Saxons would fall on barracks or encampments, on castles or shipments of coin, till the Normans were run ragged with chasing him. Elsewhere King William's Norman Conquest was quick, easy, unopposed. But in the fenlands, thanks to Brainbiter and the Saxon who wielded it, the rivers often ran red with Norman blood.

The landscape itself defied conquest. Hidden within its wet wilderness, Hereward and his men were as elusive as fish underwater. At long last, William found out that Hereward's stronghold was on the remote and moated Island of Ely. He determined, difficult as it would be, to put Hereward the "Wakeful" to sleep once and for all.

He would throw a bridge or causeway across the water, so that his army could storm the island. Of course, he needed labourers to build such a bridge, but it never occurred to him that the enemy would volunteer to help build it . . .

Hereward covered his long blond hair with a hessian hood, shouldered a bag of tools and set off to build bridges for the Normans. Day after day, he sank pilings, raised levees, knocked in nails, dug drainage trenches. He even helped build the tower at one end of the bridge, though he was not sure what it was for.

"Ah! So you are the woman I sent for," said King William, suppressing a shudder of revulsion. "Do you know your task?"

The woman in front of him ran her fingers through tangled masses of greasy, grey plaits. "I must curse the

Saxons and blast their souls to ashes." Her voice was so loud that the King involuntarily put his hands over his ears.

"Not that I believe in your magic," he said, paying her in French gold, "but these Saxons are as superstitious as fishwives. They have a horror of witches like you – and you, madam, have made an art of horror, so I hear."

The witch looked at him with contempt and fingered the mummified shrew strung round her neck. "You do your part, and I will do mine," she said.

As the causeway neared completion, William massed his forces, ready to swarm across the water into Hereward's stronghold. Shortly before dawn, the workmen were withdrawn. The French witch mounted the tower like a great black spider climbing into its web, and her ugly voice rasped out:

"A curse on you, Hereward's men! Your luck is held in a sieve! Your blood is curdling in your veins! The

hairs fallen from your head are in my cauldron! I have spoken with the spirits. I have warned the worms of your coming! My toads have walked on your faces while you slept: I know your dreams! My cat has scratched a hole for your skulls to lie in!"

Under the causeway, though no one knew it, one workman had remained behind. Hereward clung to the underside of the bridge like a crab in an upturned boat, and between his teeth was a burning fuse. He stuffed kindling into a crevice and lit it. Then he dropped down and waded, chin-deep, back to his island stronghold. The noise of the witch's insane laughter disturbed him. His men were as bold as greyhounds, but he knew what terror the black arts could strike in them. He saw their eyes glimmer in the dark, staring out at that crazy crone. Then he realized that the glimmer in their eyes was firelight. His fire had taken. The causeway was burning.

Two hundred Normans had already started across the bridge before they realized that it was alight. The witch was chanting incantations now, curses in rhyme. She worked herself to such a frenzy of abuse that she was unaware of the panic below, the splash of men jumping for their lives, the groaning of timbers breaking, the roar of fire. Gradually, an orange glare suffused the whole scene. throwing every figure into silhouette, showing the gaunt latticework of her flimsy tower.

No one gave a thought to saving the witch – William's men were too busy saving themselves. When the fire reached her, she screamed curses against Norman and Saxon alike, dancing puppet-like on an orange platform. Then, with a soughing rush of wind and ash, the burning tower listed and toppled into the river. The witch was silenced. The marsh soaked up her black magic. A constellation of burning cinders settled with a hiss on the sodden landscape.

Of course sometimes the wild places of England can be as confusing and dangerous to a Saxon as to a Norman, and more than once Hereward himself went astray. After a daring raid on Stamford, as his band made their way through Rockingham Forest, cloud blotted out the moon and left them blunderingly, helplessly lost.

All of a sudden, a gentle light began to shine ahead of him, and he glimpsed another out of the corner of his eye. Soon, individual flames – disembodied balls of light – were settling like birds on the branch of each tree. A soldier gasped and dropped his shield, but Hereward picked it up and gave it back to him. "Don't be afraid," he said. "It's just St Peter returning a favour." And no mistake, there were candles of phosphorescence glowing on every tree and shield rim – enough to see by, enough to reach a dry bed by an Anglo-Saxon hearth.

Hereward was a Lincolnshire squire, bitterly resentful of
Norman supremacy over the defeated Anglo-Saxons.
When a Norman abbot was appointed to Peterborough
Abbey (St Peter's), he did lead an attack on the abbey, by
way of a protest. Though he had been adopted as a folk-
loric hero within forty years of his death, those who wrote
about him knew few firm facts. What they did not know,
they made up, saying he was the son of Lady Godiva and
Leofric (see page 16), and crediting him with various
adventures which previously had been told about other
heroes. Some of the romance attaching to his name comes
from Charles Kingsley's novel, Hereward the Wake.

Margaret's Prayer
1070-1071

King Malcolm was not a man easily moved to pity. But when he saw Margaret, her sister and her mother, storm-soaked and exhausted, he was very moved indeed, and the feeling in his heart was nothing like pity.

A ship, bound for Hungary but driven ashore on the Scottish coast, had brought to his doorstep Edgar Aetheling, a claimant to the throne of England. The Norman conquest, rebellion and civil war had erased young Edgar's hopes of ever wearing the crown, and now he was fleeing for his life with his mother and two sisters, Christina and Margaret. Malcolm Canmore, King of Scotland, opened his door to the runaways – gave them food and shelter and warm whisky. But his eyes were always and only on Margaret, the stillness of her hands, the long-lashed lids of her downcast eyes.

Everything about Princess Margaret delighted him, from her soft psalm-singing to the Hungarian lilt of her accent. He was nearly forty and she was twenty-four. He quickly made up his mind to marry her. There was only one obstacle to overcome: Margaret was already promised in marriage: to God.

She had long since made up her mind to be a nun, and all her education had prepared her for a cloistered life. She was altogether out of place at the court of King

Malcolm, a barbarous, uncultured man who swore and drank and whose chief joy in life was to ride over the border and kill Englishmen. So her mother and sister were startled when, without explanation, Margaret the pious, Margaret the pure, suddenly abandoned her vocation and agreed to marry Malcolm Canmore.

Pleased as he was, Malcolm was baffled by his new bride. She left his bed at unearthly hours of the night; she ate like a sparrow. She no sooner had money in her purse than it was gone and she was asking for more. She even stole from him! He saw her scribble hasty notes and dispatch them furtively by rider or runner. Even in broad daylight she would often disappear – he had no idea where – creeping out of the house alone, without a word, and not returning for hours.

Malcolm began to suspect the worst. Was she meeting a lover? Was she lavishing her money on some sweetheart? Could this lady, who had been unwilling to marry and stain her purity, really be deceiving him? He vowed to find out. The very next time she slipped away down the back stairs, he followed her, at a distance, to see where she went. He followed her northwards along the winding streets of Dunfermline town. How eagerly she moved, head down, hurrying through the alleyways! At last she ducked in at the dark doorway of a low building.

Hand on knife, Malcolm followed, swearing to kill her then and there if his suspicions proved right. Already he could hear that soft sweet voice of hers whispering tenderly . . .

The place was more of a cave than a room: a gloomy, secret place. Peeping inside, Malcolm crossed himself and dodged hastily backwards, cracking his head on the arch. Smiling now, he bent for a second look.

There knelt his wife in front of a simple altar, her lips moving in fervent prayer.

"Lord God, protect and bless my beloved husband, and grant me the power to work some good upon his nature. He does not mean to be so fierce and brutal. He has a good heart underneath his shouting and cursing. Be good to him! Perhaps he has his reasons. Perhaps he does not enjoy the same happiness as I am blessed with."

Tears of remorse sprang to Malcolm's eyes. How he had misjudged his beautiful queen! Well, he would make things up to her! Perhaps with her help he could even make things up with God! Following his wife home again, he saw what became of his stolen money, too. She gave it liberally to the beggars and maimed old soldiers who haunted the lanes of Dunfermline town.

After that, the court of Malcolm Canmore was a different place. Not that the Scottish lords there were any-the-less wild or warlike, but their days followed a different course. Every morning, nine little orphans were brought to the Queen's private room so that she could sit them on her lap and feed them with her own spoon. Before every one of her own meals, the Queen would serve twenty-four poor people with food. The chamberlain had the nightly task of finding six poor people, fetching them to the castle, and making them presentable: because somewhere between a triple dose of prayers in the middle of the night and going briefly back to bed, the King and Queen liked to wash the feet of the poor, in keeping with what the Bible taught. During Lent as many as 300 needy citizens would file daily into the great hall, the doors would close, and the King and Queen in person would serve them a meal.

Monasteries and churches were built; religious men came to advise Malcolm on how to breathe new life into Scottish worship. And those hastily scribbled letters? They were indeed to spies. Margaret kept spies all over Scotland, so as to know about the English captives being held to ransom on Scottish soil. As well as ensuring that they were not cruelly treated during their captivity, she frequently paid their ransom herself.

She went on stealing gold from Malcolm's coffers; he often saw her do it. But now it made him laugh, rather than rage. His saintly little queen never ceased to amaze and astound Malcolm. Though she ate less than any of the chickens in the yard, she was tireless in her work. Furthermore, she gave birth to eight strong, healthy babies one after another, and they all lived to adulthood – a miracle indeed in those days.

One thing did not change about Malcolm's life; oddly, Margaret made no attempt to change it. She never said to Malcolm, "For the love of God or for love of me, don't go to war. Don't go raiding over the borders. Don't kill and plunder and burn . . ." Raids and wars were as much a part of her husband's life as the cut of his beard or the shoes he wore. But every day he was away, she prayed for his safe and speedy return. Even when she was ill. Even when the pain cramped her stomach like a sword thrust, she prayed for him and for his people rather than for herself.

She was ill when he set off the last time, with their oldest son, Edward. She was dying when they brought her the news that they were both dead.

If her waiting women expected Margaret to turn her face to the wall in despair – if they expected her to reproach God for rejecting her prayers, she surprised them one last time.

"All praise be to Thee Almighty God, who has been pleased that I should endure such deep sorrow at my departing, and I trust that by means of this suffering it is Thy pleasure that I should be cleansed from some of the stains of my sins." Then in the middle of reciting the Communion prayer, she simply stopped breathing.

Queen Margaret made a radical impact on eleventh-century Scotland. She was quickly declared a saint – Scotland's only royal saint – and though the account of her life by Turgot, her confessor, may exaggerate somewhat, her life patently merited sainthood. Turgot, a monk, was commissioned by Margaret's daughter (later Queen Matilda of England) to write *The Life of St Margaret*. Several miracles were reported soon after her death.

Who Killed Red Rufus?

1100

When he was ill, there was no one more religious than William Rufus. But when he was well, he was the Devil made flesh. He plundered Church coffers and jeered and sneered at its faith. Each time a church post became vacant, Rufus postponed appointing a new man – left the position empty, and took all the revenue himself. Or else he sold the post to the highest bidder. There was not one sincere religious conviction in his whole blasphemous soul. The only music which moved him was the jingle of money and the cry of the hunt.

From the people, he took the great primaeval forests, declaring all the wild life in them his to hunt. And he guarded this royal prerogative with grotesque cruelty, maiming and hanging poachers, razing villages to the ground which were in his way. It is said that the Saxon oaks groaned under slavery to this Norman tyrant. Consequently, this ruddy-faced Rufus was not a man blessed with good friends . . . nor a man short of enemies.

One summer morning in 1100, William-called-Rufus was staying in Winchester, for the hunting. After a huge breakfast, he was preparing to hunt when a fletcher, or arrow-maker, presented him with six new arrows. He admired them, passed two to his closest companion, Walter Tirel, and went outdoors to the waiting horses. As he mounted up, a letter arrived post-haste from a monastery in Gloucestershire: a letter of warning.

One of the monks had dreamed a dream: a woman kneeling in front of the throne of Christ, begging Him to free England from the yoke of King William.

The warning rolled harmless off the King's back. He just laughed, screwed up the letter, and spurred his horse to a gallop.

Once inside the forest, the huntsmen split up. William and Tirel set up on either side of a clearing, while the beaters startled a roe deer out of the undergrowth. It sprang between the two men. The King raised his crossbow to shoot, but the arrow glanced off the deer's hide. "Shoot, Walter! Shoot!" shouted the King, and Tirel fired.

With a whistle, a thud, a bolt struck William Rufus in the chest. He was dead before he hit the ground. From everywhere, men came running forward to stare at the body on the ground. Tirel knelt over it. "It wasn't me!" he said.

"The arrow's like the ones he gave you this morning," the royal huntsman pointed out. The stares were all turned on Tirel now – fixed, accusing stares. Without a word, Tirel remounted his horse and galloped south, towards Southampton. He could see that he was going to get blamed, guilty or not.

Hours later, a pair of charcoal-burners were scuffing their way through the woods collecting brushwood and dead twigs when they came across the body of the King, the triple feathers of a crossbow bolt emerging from his chest like a seedling. Of his courtiers and

huntsmen and friends – of his brother Henry – there was not a sign.

The charcoal burners bundled Rufus on to their handcart and trundled him out of the green forest gloom, jolting him over tree roots and leaving behind a trail of blood like scarlet periwinkles growing in his wake. "Him bled all the way," they told the priests at Winchester Cathedral, tipping the King out on to the stone slabs.

But no one was interested. Duke Henry was already there, at the cathedral, arguing with the bishop, trying to lay hands on the royal treasure which was kept there. He was now King, he said, the crown had passed to *him*. The argument grew noisy and undignified. The bishop maintained that William's *other* brother, Duke Robert, was the rightful heir. But Robert was away crusading – not there to defend his interests.

William Rufus, his face smeared redder than red now with his own heart's blood, lay on the flags of Winchester Cathedral and said nothing at all.

When it came to burying Rufus, the Church had its revenge. They called him an unbeliever, a heretic, a blasphemer. They called him an enemy of the Church and a sacrilegious villain. They deigned to sink him in the ground – under the floor of Winchester Cathedral, no less – but no one spoke a word of prayer over him. No one sanctified his burial or prayed for his soul.

Seven years later the cathedral tower crashed down, shattering sepulchres and statues, fonts and pulpits. Devout folk locally blamed the presence of evil Rufus.

But the people who lived by the forest saw things differently. They said that the forest, older than Christianity, had exacted a blood sacrifice, so that its crowns of green might continue to flourish. In that case, just whose hand fired the crossbow hardly matters.

William II was not the firstborn son of William the Conqueror. He raced to England from his father's deathbed in order to lay claim to it. The barons rebelled in 1088, deeming Robert the rightful king. But William was able to suppress their rebellion by appealing to the people, making them fine promises which he did not keep. These were turbulent times. He was obliged to go to war with his brother Robert, to invade Wales three times and to defend the north of the country against invasion by Malcolm III of Scotland. In fact, William the Conqueror had secured only the south of England, and it took William Rufus to complete the Norman Conquest.

The White Ship

1120

At last there was peace. After years of war between England and France, a peace had been struck, and the future blossomed with promise. King Henry I's heart was crammed with cheerful memories and optimistic plans as he boarded his ship at Barfleur, bound for England. The ship rubbed flanks with another in the harbour – *La Blanche Nef* – *the White Ship* – whose captain had begged for the honour of conveying the

King's party home. But Henry's ship was ready, laden and rigged. So, sooner than snub the good captain, Henry had entrusted his children to the *White Ship*, along with the royal treasure. They could follow on the next tide, Prince William and the rest.

Of course, as far as Henry was concerned his children were the royal treasure. He was a harsh, demanding father, not above dragging one daughter through a frozen moat to teach her a lesson; but he adored his children. His oldest son, his heir, Prince William, had grown into as fine a young man as any father could hope for. In France he had won his spurs, remembered his manners, charmed the French court. And Maud! How lovely little Maud had looked as she wished him *bon voyage*. Fortunate England that it should enjoy both peace and the promise of such princes and princesses. Fortunate Henry. The sea was calm, the sky generous and big. The King watched Barfleur slip below the horizon, then walked to the prow to watch for the Dover coast.

The tide ebbed and flowed once more. The young people of the royal party, no longer required to be on their best behaviour, drank a little too much and became noisy and excitable. When French priests came down to the waterfront to bless *La Blanche Nef*, the English crew and passengers told them in blunt, colourful English: "Take yourselves off, you sheep-faced bunch of old women!" Even so, long after the *White Ship* had set sail, one of those priests stayed on, looking out to sea, moving his lips in silent prayer. He stood there till the grey of evening turned to night.

On board the King's ship, the look-out cocked his ear and looked back southwards. Everyone heard it: a strange shrill cry carrying over the water. Gulls, they thought. Gulls, thought the King.

The *White Ship*'s eager captain, Thomas Fitz-Stephen, had set himself the task of overtaking the royal ship, proving the excellence of both ship and crew. The prow cut smartly through the waves, unslowed by cross-winds or swell. But the steersman, either drunk or ignorant of the rocky Raz de Catteville, was taking the *White Ship* to her death.

When she struck rocks submerged by high tide, the people aboard loosed a cry – a single scream of horror which travelled like cannonfire across the sea. Within minutes the vessel lay with her keel ripped open, the sea gushing in.

"Hold her to the rocks with grappling hooks!" Captain Fitz-Stephen commanded. "The rocks will hold her up till help comes!" But the rocks only chewed the ship apart, board by board.

"Get the prince away safe!" commanded the captain, and even amid the panic and confusion, one jolly-boat was got off, with Prince William kneeling up, white-faced on the rear thwart.

It was not a sight for a boy to see – his friends, his brothers, his sisters being washed one by one off the tilting deck. The noise was terrible – the howled prayers, the curses, the cries, the submerged rocks grinding on the keel. If the tide had been lower, the rocks themselves would have stuck up out of the water: somewhere to cling. But the rocks were only a darkness now below the water. Swimmers trod nothing but numbing, icy water.

"My sister! I hear my sister!" cried Prince William. "Row back! We must save Maud!" His beloved sister's screams drew him like a magnet.

The rowers did turn back. They were able to snatch Maud from where she clung to the stringy rigging sluiced by icy sea. But the water round about her was alive with swimmers. Like sharks they snatched at the oars. Hands shark-blue with cold came over the side of the boat, the drowning trying to pull themselves aboard. Desperately, the rowers tried to prise the fingers loose, but the boat rolled lower and lower . . . until the sea simply washed in over the back and sucked everything down in the foundering swirl of the *White Ship*.

Captain Fitz-Stephen, surfacing from an eternity of airless cold, grasped a broken spar to keep himself afloat. Two men erupted through the surface nearby and heaved themselves over a piece of flotsam. One was a scrawny young courtier, Geoffrey Daigle, wearing thin, torn silks, one a fat Barfleur butcher in a sheepskin jacket.

"What of the King's son? Are the King's children safe?" called the captain.

"All gone! Drowned and gone!" came the reply, and the captain, his honour already drowned in the Raz de Catteville, let go the spar and slid back down into the dark. Better to die than to live with the shame of what he had done.

Before morning the butcher of Barfleur found himself alone on the ocean, sole survivor of the wreck of the *White Ship*.

It is said that the royal treasure washed up intact on a French beach. Not so the heir to the English throne.

When the news reached England, no one knew how to tell the King. No one wanted to be the man who broke the King's heart. So they found a young boy and taught him to say the words parrot-fashion. "The *White Ship* is gone down, sire. Your children are lost."

When the King heard the words, he rose to his feet and stood silent for a few moments. Then his knees gave way, and he crashed to the ground, unconscious. It is said that King Henry I never smiled again.

Most of Henry's reign was spent in wars to retain Normandy as part of his kingdom. But at home he was a popular king, putting right much of the damage done by William Rufus. He was well advised by St Anselm whom he recalled from exile.

Prince William was his only legitimate son. After the tragedy of the *White Ship*, Henry married again in the hope of producing another heir. When no boy was born, he declared his daughter Matilda heiress to the throne, and had his barons swear allegiance to her. But after his death civil war broke out between the forces of Matilda and Stephen, another grandson of Edward the Confessor.

"This Turbulent Priest"

1170

As young men, Thomas à Becket and King Henry II were the best of friends. They were forever horsing about, vying with each other as to who wore the most splendid clothes or made the most witty remark. Once, the King had pulled off Thomas's cloak for a joke, and given it to a poor old man, telling Becket that "charity demanded it".

Thomas was only a low-born commoner, but he showed such genius at any and every job that he rose from soldier to ambassador to chancellor! Henry was happy to work hand-in-glove with clever, witty, tactful, *loyal* Thomas. He even entrusted his son's education to him.

The Church, on the other hand, was regularly troublesome to Henry. The Church felt less need to obey the King than it did God and the Pope. Henry's solution was to put someone he could trust in authority over the Church. And who better than Becket?

"I do not want the office," said Thomas. "You will take your favour from me, and our love will then become hatred."

Henry should have listened; Becket's advice had always been sound. But he brushed the warning aside. In 1162, Thomas à Becket was consecrated Archbishop of Canterbury.

He changed then. As if Henry had accidentally spoken some magic word, Becket began to alter. He resigned as chancellor, laid aside the rich clothes, the vanity and splendour of court life, and dressed like a monk, with a hair shirt against his skin. Each night, after supper, he had himself flogged, in penance for his sins. He gave away his belongings – and he gave over his loyalty – the loyalty which, till that time had belonged entirely to Henry II – to God and to the Church.

Suddenly he was the champion of the clergy, defending the Church against any and every attack. Henry found to his dismay that, far from gaining influence over the Church, he was being thwarted at every turn by Archbishop Becket. Henry felt betrayed. Becket's former friends and colleagues felt betrayed.

The two men clashed most fiercely when Henry tried to make the clergy answerable to the law. At that time, a priest could rob or murder or burn down a house and still escape arrest. Extraordinarily, Becket refused to give up this much-abused privilege. Henry retaliated by confiscating castles and fining Becket for leaving his post as chancellor. He took his son out of Becket's care.

On the day the King's pages threw mud at him and called him "Traitor!", Becket realized the danger he was in, and took a ship for France. For two years the cold Channel flowed between the two friends, and a still colder hostility.

Then the quarrel was patched up and Becket came home. The nobility still resented him, but not the common people. He was one of them! He was a saintly man who daily washed the feet of the poor! They had tasted his charity, his goodness, his sanctity! They welcomed him home like a conquering hero, thronging

Canterbury in the hope of glimpsing the great man.

Becket had not mellowed in the least. He was as pious and as unyielding as ever. Now he began to wield a power even Henry did not possess. He began to excommunicate his enemies.

A king can cut off a man's head, but the man's soul is free to fly up to heaven. An archbishop – by snuffing out a candle, ringing a bell, closing a book – can condemn a man's soul to burn in everlasting fire. How could Henry compete with that kind of power?

Far away, in his French territories, Henry raged at Becket's insolence, pride and thanklessness. "A fellow that has eaten my bread! A fellow that came to court on a lame horse with a cloak for a saddle!" He fumed and fulminated. His chair turned over, and he began to pace the room, throwing his hands about in melodramatic gestures, smacking at his forehead, groaning and gasping with exasperation. "What cowards have I brought up in my court, who care nothing for their duty to their master! Will no one rid me of this turbulent priest?"

Four knights – Sir Reginald Fitzurse, Sir Richard le Breton, Sir Hugh de Merville and Sir William Tracy – looked at one another, got up and left the room. They sailed to England that night.

They rode to Canterbury Cathedral with a band of horsemen, but went inside alone, unarmed. Naturally. It is a sacrilege to wear a sword inside a church.

Becket kept them waiting. When he finally deigned to see them, there were heated words behind closed doors, and then an argument which spilled out into public.

"We bring you the commands of the King . . . Will

you come with us to the King and account for yourself?"

"I will not."

"Absolve the bishops you excommunicated!"

"I will not!"

Their voices rang up and down the echoing cloisters of the huge building. "In that case, the King's final demand is that you depart out of this realm and never return!"

"I do not choose to go. Nothing but death shall part me from my Church!"

At that moment, the bell began to ring for vespers. The great cathedral stirred itself for divine service. The nave would be filling with townspeople. The sounds of holy ritual chased the knights outside into the late afternoon. There they threw off their white cloaks – and began buckling on swords.

A friend of Becket's, who had witnessed the argument, shook his head anxiously. "My lord Archbishop, it is a pity you will never be advised. You would have done far better to have kept quiet and answered them mildly."

But Becket was in no mood for advice or soft words. He set out along the cloisters, towards the cathedral, to conduct vespers – found he had left his cross behind – would not go on till it was fetched. Monks flitted past in alarmed disorder. "They are arming!"

"Let them arm. Who cares?" Those were Becket's exact words.

The monks wanted to lock the cathedral doors – they had already locked the hall door.

"I will not have the church turned into a castle," said Becket irritably.

Meanwhile, finding the hall doors locked against them, the four knights could have gone round to the main entrance and got in easily, but they dragged a ladder over to a window and broke in that way, hurrying through the building, hard on the heels of Becket.

Daylight was all but gone. The only light in the nave came from banks of tallow candles: lozenges of gold floating in the cavernous dark. Some monks had run and hidden. Others were determined to protect their archbishop, even if it cost them their lives. "What are you afraid of?" asked Becket, annoyed by their busy comings and goings.

"Where is the traitor? Where is Thomas Becket?" *Becket-ket-ket.* It echoed round the nave. No one answered.

"Where is the archbishop . . . *ishop . . . ishop?*"

That title Becket was ready to acknowledge. "I am here."

Fitzurse had never meant this to happen. He owed so much to Becket. In a low quick whisper he said: "Flee, or you are a dead man."

"I am ready to die. And may the Church, through my death, obtain peace and liberty. I charge you in the name of God that you hurt no one here but me."

There was a noise of running feet: townspeople had heard there was something amiss and began flocking up the nave now, only to find a man with a sword barring their way to the choir. The darkness added to the confusion.

Fitzurse suddenly grabbed Becket and tried to drag him away. Perhaps he still thought to take the archbishop prisoner and avoid bloodshed. But Becket tore loose: "Off, Reginald. Touch me not!"

Then Tracy and le Breton were on him. But Thomas was tall and strong: he threw Tracy to the ground. He called Fitzurse a Judas. Again Fitzurse told him to run. Again Becket refused. In a clumsy muddle of movements, Fitzurse waved his sword and knocked off Becket's mitre; perhaps he was still trying to frighten him. A monk tried to fend off the second, heavy, downward blow, but fell to his knees as the blade broke his arm, and cut deep into Becket's head. A third stroke felled Thomas to his knees, hands raised as if in prayer.

For a moment all was stillness: a candlelit silence. Then Becket keeled over on to his face, with no more noise than a cloak makes in falling from a man's shoulders.

A fourth blow scalped him. The most vicious wound of all was made last, through the open wound. They made very sure the "turbulent priest" was dead.

When Europe heard the news, it quaked like a drumskin. The primate of England murdered in his own cathedral on the orders of his King?

When Henry heard the news, he gasped and wept inconsolably. What a terrible mistake, he cried. His words had been misunderstood! He had never meant

54

his old friend to be murdered!

When he got back to England, he took off his royal clothes and walked barefoot to Canterbury Cathedral in a hair shirt and pilgrim's cloak, to kiss the flagstones where his friend had died. Beside the tomb, he fell weeping on his face and allowed each one of the eighty bishops and monks to lash him with whips: five lashes each.

The watching thousands crowding the streets of Canterbury were impressed. Nothing less would have satisfied them, but they were impressed.

Quite soon there came news of miracles bestowed by the dead archbishop. Pilgrims began to converge on Canterbury from all over the country. After all, Becket the martyr was an easier man to love than Becket the cantankerous archbishop. And the common people had a new voice to speak for them in heaven: a man low-born like themselves, their very own saint.

BECKET'S SHRINE

Becket, though of Norman blood, was actually born in London, and in that respect was the first Englishman to hold important state office after the Norman Conquest of 1066. This was part of the reason the common people adored him. They saw him as a buffer between them and the French-Norman nobility. He was declared a saint in 1173, and Henry made his penance in 1174.

But none of the four murderers was punished . . . So perhaps they had not misunderstood King Henry's words so completely, after all.

The Fair Rosamond

about 1175

Eleanor of Aquitaine was a woman who had gone to the Crusades, worn eastern robes in the palaces of Constantinople, captured the hearts of a hundred troubadours and broken them all by marrying a second husband, this time for love.

But Henry II was ten years younger than she, and a man of such immoderate passions that, in his tempers, he bit men's shoulders or fell on his face and chewed the straw. It was unlikely, from the very outset, that he would ever give his love to Eleanor alone.

He had a whole gaggle of lovers, but none took so firm a hold on his heart as Rosamond Clifford, known as the Fair Rosamond.

Some said that they had been sweethearts since childhood days, and that Henry had secretly married Rosamond before he ever met Queen Eleanor. But whatever the truth, Henry determined to keep Rosamond both secret from the Queen and hidden from any eyes but his. So he shut her up – a willing captive – somewhere he was sure the Queen would never find her, and he visited her as often as he was in Oxfordshire. Perhaps the Queen suspected. Perhaps she kept watch. Or perhaps it was by chance that she saw Henry striding out one day across his estates at Woodstock Park, and spotted something trailing from his heel. His spur had snagged a thread of silk, and as he walked towards the house, it pulled taut behind him. Where had he been, to have embroidery thread caught around his spur?

He did not see Eleanor standing in the shade of a tree, and when he had passed by, she stepped out and picked up the thread, following it back in the direction the King had come. Through the vegetable garden it ran, around a bush, across a grassy lawn to the maze.

It was notoriously huge and complex, the maze Henry had designed to ornament his park; a knot of paths circling and doubling back on themselves. Eleanor had never entered it, for she was a busy woman and could not spare time on such idle amusements. But she entered it now.

The paths wound to and fro until, without the thread to guide her, Eleanor would have been hopelessly lost. But the strand of blood-red silk led her unerringly to the centre, and at the centre she found a door. Through the door she went, down stairs into a

subterranean passageway which twisted as intricately below ground as the maze had done above. She was not bewildered by the dark and twisting corridors, for she had the thread in her hand. She had long since guessed what she would find at her journey's end.

Soon a glimmer of light showed ahead of her, and the passage opened into a large, well-lit room hung with tapestries. A beautiful young woman with yellow hair leaned intently over her embroidery; at her feet a basket of silks, the red skein half pulled out and unravelled almost to its end. The sewer looked up, thinking that Henry had for-gotten something and returned. Her lovely face registered first shock, then fear, then a slightly proud defiance.

"Tell me your name," demanded the Queen.

"I am Rosamond Clifford, ma'am."

"Are you held prisoner here against your will?"

"Oh no, ma'am! It is my joy and duty to –"

But Eleanor had turned her back – gone. Within half an hour she had returned. In the meantime,

Rosamond's courage had risen. "Did you ask him? Did Henry tell you? We were married these many years since, and have a son true-born and –"

"I will ask you again," Eleanor interrupted. "Are you held prisoner here against your will?"

"I told you before," said Rosamond. "I am not."

"In that case, you are free to go," said the Queen. She took out from a pouch at her belt a little Turkish dagger, souvenir of the Crusades, also a small bottle of some blue-green liquid. "Shall you die by the dagger or by the poisoned cup? For die you shall, Fair Rosamond, and with you your shame and the shame of my husband, King of England."

There was no crying out, no appealing to Henry to overrule his wife; they were far from the house and deep underground. "Nothing you can do will alter the fact that Henry loves me best!" said Rosamond through her tears. "Nothing in any of your apothecary's bottles will ever serve to make you young again, nor blot out the truth – that you were married first to King Louis and abandoned him so as to be Queen of England! I *love* Henry! I have always loved Henry – not his country, not his title! And Henry loves me. So which of us do you think is his *true* wife?"

But it was fruitless to argue with Eleanor about love. Eleanor knew all about love. Leaving the house, she locked the door behind her. Leaving the maze, she sheathed the little Turkish dagger. For Rosamond had chosen the poison in preference to the blade. Even now she lay amid her tapestries and silks with an empty cup in her hand and a thread of spilled wine amid her yellow hair.

Rosamond Clifford may well have married Henry when he was a boy; he once swore that their son was legitimate. But whether and however Eleanor discovered her husband's secret love, the part about the poison and the dagger never happened. Rosamond died much later at Godstow Abbey near Oxford, where she had been living for many years. Perhaps Eleanor obliged her to enter the convent.

Eleanor of Aquitaine continued to be a sore trial to her husband in all kinds of ways. She tended to support his enemies and favour her sons before her husband. But given their natures, it must have been an extraordinary marriage.

The mazes built in those days would have been elaborate, raised-turf patterns, not the obscuring kind with high hedges, so the story of the thread is also probably a fiction.

The Troubadour Rescues His King

1193

"Hail, King of England, in vain you disguise yourself. Your face betrays you." As Richard awoke, it was a moment before he could remember where he was, or what had brought him to be captured at sword point in this dirty, ill-lit room which smelled of ale. Then it came back to him – his eventful homeward voyage from the Holy Land, his landfall on unfriendly shores, his attempt to reach home, disguised as a peasant. Now, in this flea-ridden inn, alone and friendless in exceedingly dangerous times, he had fallen into the hands of Duke Leopold of Austria.

Richard had made enemies of half the crowned heads of Europe. They tussled over him like dogs over a bone. Duke Leopold waited to see who would offer most for his prestigious prisoner. His enemies either wanted to ransom Richard for cash, or to kill him. His brother, Prince John, was longing to hear that Richard had died on his way home so that he could seize the crown of England. If news could be kept quiet of Richard's capture, there was a chance he would moulder away in some obscure dungeon and never reappear.

Fortunately, the truth got free. Rumours of the

King's capture spread far and wide: somewhere the King of England, Richard the Lion-Hearted, lay in chains, his only hope the persistence of his friends in seeking him out.

Blondel was a troubadour – a writer of ballads, a singer of roundelays. Richard was partial to music and verse and to handsome young men. He had encouraged and rewarded Blondel, and Blondel was, in return, devoted to his king. As soon as he heard Richard was missing, he vowed he would travel the world until he had found him.

Day after week after month the troubadour roamed Europe, earning his bread with a song, sleeping under the stars. A musician could go anywhere. So long as Blondel was careful whom he questioned and how many questions he asked, he would not arouse suspicion. And if he kept his eyes open and listened carefully in the alehouses and market squares, he was sure he could track Richard down.

Eighteen months later, having found no trace or whisper of an imprisoned king, he was less sure.

At last, just when he was on the point of despair, he struck up conversation with an innkeeper's wife. She said: yes, there was a rumour – it might only be gossip – you know how people talk – but up at the castle – that gloomy place, aye, up yonder by the river – she had heard tell there was a prisoner locked up in the tower who was of such importance that the duke guarded him day and night. Tall, people said he was, with the kind of clothes the angels in heaven would wear if they could afford them. Blondel feigned a mild interest and bent his head low over his lute, tuning its strings . . .

As soon as he could get away without attracting attention, he climbed the road to the castle, meandered through the open gates. Taking up a position at the foot of the tower, he began to sing, loudly and brightly.

Pigmen at the sties, squires at the tilt, ladies  embroidering at their windows all glanced curiously in his direction. It was not unusual for troubadours to travel about the countryside singing for their supper, and it made a pleasant interlude in the forbidding silence of brooding Castle Dürrenstein. Blondel's sweet voice echoed off the wall and came back at him, mocking. He shifted his ground to the other side of the tower, and sang again.

Slumped in his cell, his wrists shackled by long chains, assailed by the smell of the slop pail and his warders' feet, Richard Coeur de Lion fumbled his way out of a dream.

He had dreamed he was in England again, singing a duet with dear Blondel. The pain of finding himself still imprisoned in his cell was as sharp as ever. The singing had stopped.

Blondel's singing had caught the attention of the castle keeper, a young knight with a large retinue of musicians and entertainers. The troubadour's voice and appearance were most agreeable, and time hangs heavy for a knight in times of peace. There was great prestige to be had from entertaining an accomplished troubadour, so he invited Blondel to join his retinue. Blondel accepted at once. It would give him time to delve deeper into the castle's secrets.

For several weeks Blondel sang and wrote verse and indulged in witty conversation with the castle staff, though to no effect. They gave nothing away. Perhaps they knew nothing. Perhaps he was wasting his time in the wrong place, while Richard lay rotting somewhere else entirely . . .

Richard, who paced his cell endlessly to exercise his legs, looked out of the window, tormented to see other men walking free. The roses in the keeper's garden were just coming into bloom. He watched them, recalling the dog-roses in the English hedgerows. The knight was out enjoying his rose garden, too. With him were all his foolish, fashionable hangers-on – pretty boys every one of them. Suddenly Richard gripped the bars and his cheeks scraped against their rusty metal. Could it be? Could it possibly be?

Richard knew he must not call out, must not draw attention to Blondel if he were there incognito. But oh! They were turning away – moving out of the garden! How to signal Blondel without endangering his life?

Richard cleared his throat. He had had no cause to sing for a year and a half, but now he began a song – a song he and Blondel had sung together a dozen times, a song he had no difficulty in remembering.

"If everything were as I wish it,
We would not divided be;
He in the east and I in the west
And in between, the sea."

Smiling despite himself, he fixed his eyes on his troubadour's face and willed him to hear.

A spasm passed through Blondel, which he hid with a sneeze. Unwrapping his lute from its cloth bag, he began to strum it. Supplying the chords at first, then joining in the descant of the song floating down from the tower, he moved away little by little from the group of squires and jongleurs. He was singing louder now, joining in split harmony with the singer in the tower, just as he had done a dozen times sitting at Richard's feet.

"The time until his ship comes home,
Is time most pitiful to me;
He in the east and I in the west,
And in between, the sea."

When the song ended, Blondel calmly wrapped up his lute again and sauntered back to the others. Tomorrow he would tell the knight that he was leaving – on a pilgrimage or a Crusade. Then he would quit Castle Dürrenstein and head for England.

He knew now where the King was being held. Prince

John might try to persuade the people his brother had died, but Blondel knew differently. He could tell the churchmen and barons and ministers and diplomats where to find their true king. All the way home, that knowledge gave rise to new songs which the troubadour sang to the seagulls from the deck of the cross-Channel packet.

Although it is true the Duke of Austria captured Richard and imprisoned him at Dürrenstein, the King was soon moved to Castle Triefels in Germany where he was tried and offered freedom in exchange for an astronomical ransom. Great doubt has to be cast on the truth of the Blondel legend, though the troubadour probably was part of Richard's retinue. £100,000 was raised in ransom – a sum which beggared England after years already spent financing Richard's crusading. The Lion Heart, spoiled, reckless, full of vices and never home, was hardly his country's best friend.

The Three Outlaws
about 1200

The men of the North Country could not come to terms at all with King John's claim to own the Forest of Englewood. It is one thing to say that the cows in a field belong to the farmer who raised them. It is quite another to say that the deer, the partridge, the wild pig and rabbits belong to one man, simply because he says so. The men of the borderlands continued to hunt there as their fathers and grandfathers had always done.

But the sheriff and justice of Carlisle were eager to prove themselves loyal officers of the King, so they hanged one man after another for killing the King's deer.

Sooner than hang, accused men slipped away into the forest and lived as outlaws, never able to visit their homes or families again. And the three bravest who ever took shelter under the greenwood trees were Adam Bell, Clym of the Cleugh, and William Cloudeslee.

One night, by the campfire, William said, "It's half a year since I saw my wife and children. Tomorrow I think I'll take a walk into Carlisle Town and pay them a visit."

"Don't be a fool, Will!" exclaimed Adam. "The sheriff has your house watched! It's too dangerous. Doesn't the little pig-boy bring you messages from home? Be content!"

But Will's mind was made up. He mingled among the last travellers of the day and arrived just before the city gates shut for the night, making his way from shadow to shadow, to rap on the shutters of his house. His wife's pale face appeared at the window.

"Will! Are you mad? What a risk to come here!" But she slipped the latch, and Will Cloudeslee was once again in his wife's arms, his children dangling from his belt and wrists and jerkin. He could hardly credit how much and how little things had changed. Alice was as beautiful as ever. His children had grown so big! Old Meg still sat by the fire.

"She's *still* here?" Will whispered.

"Of course! You said she could stay, when she had nowhere else to go. She took you at your word!" Alice whispered, laughing. "She's part of the furniture now."

Will greeted the old lady by the fire, asked after her health, then turned his attention to his family.

Everyone thought Old Meg was bed-ridden; a harmless, helpless old woman. So they never thought she could slip out of her shadowy corner, out of the house and away down the alley. Never for a moment did it occur to them that a guest treated with such kindness might betray them for a quick profit. Old Meg went straight to the sheriff. "If I give into your hands that outlaw William Cloudeslee, what will you give me?"

Old Meg sold Will to his enemies for a piece of scarlet cloth, then creeping back to her place by the fire, she sat with the parcel crammed under her dress, warming her wicked knees.

At around midnight, Alice glanced out of the window, and saw the glimmer of chain mail. Armed men. "You are betrayed, Will," she said. "Run!"

But it was too late. The sheriff's men surrounded the building and there was nothing for it but to stay and fight, or surrender and be taken. "Get into the bedroom," said Alice picking up an axe. "I'll guard the door while you use your bow."

Will looked at her across the heads of their children. "I do not deserve you," he said.

The sheriff sneered when he saw his best men running to shelter from Will's flying arrows. "Burn the place down! That will put an end to his archery."

The town's people, brought from their beds by the commotion, gave a roar of protest as they saw burning faggots stacked against the house. "What about the man's children? What about his wife? For shame!"

The sheriff simply narrowed his eyes against the smoke, covered his nose against the stench of burning.

Will fought on till the sound of his children's crying blinded his own eyes with tears. "I won't have your lives on my conscience!" he called to Alice. "Pull the sheets off the bed and tear them in strips . . ."

Alice would have chosen to stay with her husband, but for the sake of her children she allowed Will to lower them all to safety down ropes of knotted sheets. The people in the street rushed forward in such numbers to help them down that the sheriff's archers were knocked off their feet. The burning house overhung them like a breaking wave of fire.

Remembering Old Meg, Will ran to save her, too. But the old crone only boggled at him, with mad, soot-rimmed eyes, and clutched a parcel to her stomach. She would not let it go – not even to put her arms around his neck. Back he ran to the window, firing arrows till the flames singed and broke the bowstring. Then he stepped out on to the sill. So much chain mail was gathered in the street below that it looked like silver sea into which he leapt . . .

"Who is the gallows for?" the little pig-boy asked the morning watchman.

"For William Cloudeslee, the outlaw," came the response.

The boy ran with the news all the way to the greenwood. "Adam Bell! Clym of the Cleugh! Where are you?" Then, crouched by the camp fire, he told them their friend was condemned to hang at noon.

"That doesn't give us long," said Adam thoughtfully. "Can you get us into Carlisle, boy?"

"Not till the gates open again! The sheriff has ordered them kept shut till Will is dead!"

"Ah, but they will open for a *King's messenger*, I know," said Clym, whose plan was already taking shape. "You and I, Adam, shall pretend to be messengers bearing a letter for the sheriff. There's only one small difficulty . . ."

"What? The guard? The gatekeeper?" Adam was eager to help.

"No. The fact that I'm not a *writing* kind of man."

Fortunately, Adam Bell could both read and write. With a tree stump for his table, he penned an impressive-looking letter which they rolled up and sealed with candle-tallow. Forest bark served in place of the royal seal. "A fitting seal for a king who thinks he owns the forest," said Adam Bell.

"No one enters until the outlaw is dead," said the gatekeeper for the third time.

"Then you'd best tell the hangman to prepare for a second hanging!" roared Adam Bell, "for by this hand, the King will have you hanged if you delay his messengers another minute!"

The gatekeeper blenched. He looked at the letter they wagged in his face, but he was not a reading sort of man, and he could not have told the royal seal from a lump of candle-tallow. So he opened up, and the two men strode in.

As he went to hang the keys back inside the gatehouse, an arm circled his throat and a hand relieved him of the keys. The "King's messenger" he had just admitted said, "I think I shall be gatekeeper of Carlisle today, and you shall be Clym of the Cleugh. Bind him, Adam, and see that he doesn't escape."

William was carried to the gallows bound hand and foot, lying face down in the execution cart. The streets were full of angry murmurings. "What has the man done but shoot a deer? Shame on the sheriff for his spite! Shame on the justice for his heartlessness!"

William was lifted to his feet, and a noose placed around his neck. The ropes round his ankles were freed so that he could climb the ladder to the gallows. The sheriff of Carlisle stood at his window rubbing his hands with glee. Beside him stood the justice, saying, "One fewer outlaw to trouble the King's deer . . ."

Those were the last words he spoke. Two arrows flew across the town square and plunged into the hearts of both sheriff and justice.

Then chaos. Adam cut Will's bonds, and Clym cleared a path across the square with his sword. The guards, slow to realize what was happening, had to push the crowds aside to give chase through the narrow streets. Under their feet they found the city pigs, let loose from their sties to trip them up. The three outlaws had plenty of time to unlock, open, close and relock the city gate. They stood on the outside breathless and laughing.

Clym slung the keys over the top of the gate. "I resign as gatekeeper!" he called. "I think I'll go back to an honest profession as outlaw!"

When they reached Englewood they found a visitor in their camp. She stood amid the green-clothed men, children clinging to her skirts, weeping as if her heart were broken. "And all for my sake!" they heard her say.

"Alice?" said Will Cloudeslee.

She stared at him as if he might be a ghost. "But I thought . . . I thought you must be dead!"

"Who, me? Never!" Then he drew his wife aside, kissed her and made her this promise. "Go home, my love. Wait for me seven years, and I shall return to you a pardoned man. Adam and Clym and I shall go to London and win the King's forgiveness. Until then, Alice, keep me alive in your thoughts and prayers, and I shall keep to the greenwood like the nightingale keeps to the tree – out-of-sight but singing, my dear, out-of-sight but singing."

Clym of the Cleugh is the borderland Robin Hood. Many of the adventures of the three outlaws overlap with those told about Robin, and Will Cloudeslee, in shooting an apple off his son's head, manages to absorb the William Tell story too. The three may well have been based on real local men, however. Outlawry was common enough in King John's reign. John's seizure of the great forests as his own personal hunting grounds caused untold suffering to the peasantry.

Cuckoos

about 1212

The King's own messengers were accustomed to causing a stir. Usually, when they rode into a town or village, people rushed out of doors to stare, local dignitaries hurried to fawn and flatter them, the inn prepared a splendid supper. But when King John's messengers rode into Gotham, nobody paid the smallest notice.

Four men came quarrelling down the road carrying between them a great length of picket fence. "It's your fault," said one.

"Well, how was I to know?"

At a shout from the royal messengers, the men with the fence all bumped into each other and stumbled to a halt. "We been trying to catch the cuckoo up yonder," explained one. "Sings in that bush on the hill. Pretty as a picklejar."

The man behind him joined in: "We knocked in this fence right around it! Got that bush so surrounded there was no getting out . . ."

"We had him, didn't we? We had him surrounded!" said a third eagerly.

"Then the cuckoo up and flew off," said the fourth sorrowfully dabbing his eyes.

King John's messengers looked at one another. One tapped his forehead with one finger. "You, sirs, are cuckoos yourselves if you didn't think of that . . ." began the chief messenger. But he was left talking to himself as the four cuckoo-catchers bumbled away down the road.

A man without trousers and wearing a jacket with wet coat-tails came sprinting down the street holding a big eel at arm's length. Dashing straight past without so much as a glance at the King's messengers, he ran to the village pond and threw the eel into it with a triumphant shout of, "There now! Drown and good riddance to you!"

Intrigued, the messengers asked what had happened. The villager looked at them with a slightly crazed grin and said, "I'm sorry you had to see that, but the vile beastie ate all the fish in our lake. So we held a trial and found it guilty and condemned it to death-by-drowning. That there was the execution."

"But eels can" – The royal messenger did not finish. Clearly the man was a lunatic if he thought he could drown eels – just as his neighbours were lunatics if they thought . . .

A woman carrying a bag of oatmeal came bustling out of the inn, calling back over her shoulder: "I'm just off down to the river to cook your porridge, Jack!" She curtsied as she passed the troupe of royal messengers. "River's bubbling nicely this morning!" she observed (as someone might comment cheerily on the weather). "Must be right hot to bubble like that! Porridge will be cooked in no time." They could not help noticing that her ears were painted green.

"They're all mad!" whispered the banner-bearer. "Are they dangerous, do you think?"

"You, sir! Come hither!" called the chief messenger imperiously. "You, farmer!"

"Oo? Me, sirrah?" A farmer leading a sway-backed old horse out of town, with two bags of grain slung across the saddle, shot them a hunted, guilty look and started talking before they could stop him. "I know what you're going to say! I know, and it's all true! This old horse shouldn't have to carry those heavy sacks, should she? Not after the lifetime of service she's given me! Well, neither shall she, sirs! Neither shall she! I'll spare her! You have showed me I am a cruel and unfeeling man!" So saying, he tugged the sacks off the old horse and tucked one under each arm. "I'll carry them myself, so I will!" Then he clambered awkwardly astride the animal's back, still clutching the sacks, and clicked his tongue for her to walk on.

"Let us hurry back and tell the King. This is no fit place for him! The village is full of half-wits! I swear there's not a soul living here but he's mad!" And so the royal messengers left at a gallop, sleeping in the forest sooner than stay in Gotham overnight.

When they had gone, the good gentlemen of Gotham converged on the Cuckoo Bush Inn for a pint or two of ale. "Reckon that put paid to them," said Farmer Giles.

"Reckon it did," said the carpenter.

"No hunting lodge hereabouts for King John, then," said the innkeeper's wife, brushing oatmeal off her dress. Everyone spat on the floor in unison.

"No Gothamites banned from their own forest, just so some king can enjoy his sport in sole splendour," said the man busy wiping the smell of eel off his hands.

"There's wisdom in what you say," said the innkeeper's wife with a wink. "But then Gotham was always blessed with a wealth of wise men."

The so-called "wise men" of Gotham first appeared in Andrew Boorde's sixteenth-century book, *Merrie Tales of the Mad Men of Gotham*, but were the stuff of folk legend before then. It has been suggested that the original wise men only feigned madness to dissuade King John from building a hunting lodge locally and annexing the surrounding forest for his own private hunting. This would have caused them very real hardship.

There are about twenty different, comic lunacies attributed to them, including trying to rescue the moon from a pond – a story the Moonrakers of Wiltshire would almost certainly have known.

Lost in the Wash

1216

Perhaps if he had been more handsome, more successful, more popular, King John would have minded less about clothes and jewellery. As it was, he carried his wealth of showy possessions with him everywhere he went. Even when the King of Scotland invaded and John set out to fight him, he took with him a baggage train of personal belongings, including the Crown Jewels.

Pushing too far south, into the Cambridgeshire fens, the Scottish invaders overreached themselves; John was easily able to turn them back, without heavy loss of men. But it left him in inhospitable fenland – a damp, shivering landscape which he hated. He had been feeling unwell lately, which made him even more irritable and impatient to get home. The sooner he and his men marched north and inland to Nottingham, the happier he would be.

And there at his feet, invitingly flat and golden,

lay the vast sands of the Wash, a bite-shaped indent in the eastern coast of England. John studied the map. "If we cut across here," he said, drawing a jewelled finger across the Wash, we can take fifty miles off our journey and be out of this pestilential county by nightfall."

So out on to the hard-packed sand threaded a long line of horses and carts, banners, dogs and wagons. John slouched in his saddle: this salt air would be ruining the vellum of his books and the silver-gilt embroidery on his robes. A vast mackerel sky gave an impression of rippling water overhead. There was spray in the air, such as marks the turn of the tide.

Some of the wagons were having difficulties – sinking into the wet sand, bogging down. The sandy, featureless plain grew more beautiful by the minute, with little twisted cords of silver, and a bluey tinge reflected from the sky. It was no longer clear where the beach ended and the sky began. The horses' hoof prints were filling with water, making a line of silver stitches across the brocade tan of the sands.

Then the mist came down – a white pall of water droplets which hung on the men's eyelashes and beards and wetted them to the skin. The distant cottages on which they had taken a bearing dissolved like lumps of sugar in milk, and the gulls fell suddenly silent.

A horse floundered and fell to its knees. Its back arched as though it were leaping invisible fences, but its feet did not move – could not move. Soon only its head was straining and tossing, while the quicksand swallowed it up. A cart turned over with a crash of breaking crockery.

The tide did not roll in. It seemed to well up from below ground. The orderly line of troops and baggage carts broke up in panic. More horses pitched nose-down, their riders flying, hands-out, into the soft, receiving sand. Suddenly they could barely hear one another above the noise of the sea. "Look to the Crown Jewels!" shouted King John. "Look to my royal treasure!"

But men were running for dry land now (though they could not see it), jumping from island to island of damp sand, while the channels in between became wider and deeper. Soon there were no more dry patches, and the soldiers were all knee-deep and floundering, the sea pushing against their thighs, dragging the sand from under their boots. Here and there, groups of men trapped by quicksand bawled for help, but the sea piled up behind them, filling up the bottom segment of the sky.

The carts were afloat now, mostly on their sides. They banged against the horses, and mounted knights cursed and abandoned them. The sea came looting its way through the bags and baggage of the royal party, snatching here a coronet, there a jewelled glove. It leafed through the pages of the King's library. Chests too heavy with gold to float bubbled pearls of air, then sank underwater and into the sand. Gold chains looped and knotted themselves to the seaweed, and gem stones glistened in one last brilliant cascade before joining all the other, unremarkable pebbles on the seabed.

The loss gripped at John's chest so hard that he thought his heart was failing. Every time he thought of his ermine and scarlet wool, he groaned with physical pain. Dozens of good men had disappeared without reaching the shore, and the survivors sat about, shocked and shivering. But John thought of each piece of beautiful treasure, the buying of it, the price he had paid, the exquisite craftsmanship, the pleasure it had given him – and misery made him clutch his stomach and howl like a dog.

They pushed on to Nottingham, where John consoled himself by gorging on preserved peaches and cider. Within a fortnight, he was dead of dysentery, unmissed and unmourned, with an epitaph which damned him as "the worst King in English history".

King John's disastrous shortcut across the Wash took place only a year after his unwilling signing of the Magna Carta. The accident was recorded many years later, by one Matthew Paris, who undoubtedly exaggerated. But since much of the royal treasure catalogued before 1216 cannot be traced, there may well be some truth in the story.

Despite his reputation for greed, cruelty and cowardice, King John was a hard-working king in England, unlike his brother Richard, who saw the territory simply as a source of revenue for his crusading. Despite the popular image of John as an oafish brute who could neither read nor write, he was a fastidiously clean, cultured, intelligent man who possessed a large library of books. He travelled the country checking on the honesty of his officials.

"Wrap Me Up In A Cloak of Gold"

1255

Two dozen boys were playing football with a pig's bladder. Someone skied the ball. It flew high over a wall, then they heard it bounce ringingly on the paved courtyard inside. Both teams scattered.

"What about my ball?" called little Sir Hugh. "I want it back!"

"Not going in there!" his friends shouted as they ran.

"Mother said to keep away!"

"A fairy lives there, says mine!"

Hugh, too, was afraid of the beetling stone walls and the big dark mansion beyond. But he stayed rooted to the spot, thinking about his ball. A gate creaked. A lady came out. She was dark-haired and beautiful, with a fine aquiline nose and dark eyes. He noticed that her gown was green – the colour fairies wear: an unlucky colour – but she smiled pleasantly enough. "Come in, little Sir Hugh. Come in and fetch your ball."

"I can't! I won't!" he blurted. "I mustn't! Not without my friends." His own rudeness embarrassed him, but the lady took no offence. She simply reached out, took Hugh by the hand and led him indoors. The gate banged shut behind them.

She smiled while he fetched his ball, smiled while he apologized for his rudeness. "Would you like some sherbet, Hughie?" she asked.

She led the way along stone corridors, through wood-panelled rooms hung with tapestries. At last they came to a windowless chamber lit by candles. "Sit down, Hughie. See, there is a golden chair for you to sit on."

"I should be going."

"Ah, but have some sweets before you go. Boys like sweets." She held out to him a plate of sugar bonbons, and he sat in the ornate golden chair, his feet swinging clear of the ground. The sweets were good . . . but they made him sleepy – they, or the incense burning in the room, or the soft glimmer of the candles. He only screamed when he saw the knife.

"No use screaming," said the lady in the same soft voice. "The walls here are a yard thick. No one will hear you." She scooped him up out of the chair as easily as if he were a baby, and laid him face-up on her dressing-table. Sleep, like a dozen strong hands, stopped him struggling.

"Let me say my prayers, at least!" he whispered.

But she stabbed him, then and there, in the throat, so that the blood ran down. The football, rolling out of his hands, bounced – tch tch tch – down a flight of stone steps. Sinking her fingers in his golden hair, gripping both ankles in one large hand, she carried him to the well by the high wall, and dropped him down it.

When little Sir Hugh did not return home, his mother went looking for him. His friends told her about the football and helped her search, sorry now that they had run off and left their friend alone. The town watch called at the big dark mansion behind its high perimeter wall, but the lady there only smiled pleasantly: no, she had not seen the boy.

His mother became more and more distracted. The river was dragged; the huntsmen checked their traps in the greenwood. But there was no trace of the boy. Then a servant lad, passing by the well, heard singing without knowing where it came from:

> *"Mother, mother, make my bed.*
> *Make for me a winding sheet.*
> *Wrap me up in a cloak of gold.*
> *See if I can sleep."*

The lad stopped passers-by: "Listen: can you hear that?"

Hugh's mother came and listened, white-faced, by the well, her hands clasped over her mouth to contain her terror.

> *"Mother, mother, make my bed.*
> *Make for me a winding sheet*
> *Wrap me up in a cloak of gold.*
> *See if I can sleep."*

The body was grappled up from the bottom of the well and given a Christian burial wearing a cloak of gold. The well fell silent then, though no one dared drink from it. Many more ball games were played up against the high stone wall, but never again was a lost ball retrieved. Never again did the lady in green open her gate and invite a child in – for she had been tried for murder and burned to dust in the market place, along with all her kith and kin.

Although this horror story features an evil fairy, it started life as a piece of anti-Jewish propaganda in which the murderer was a Jew. The ritual murder in 1255 of nine-year-old Hugh of Lincoln was the reason given for hanging several (probably innocent) Jewish men in the city. The thirteenth century was a time of great religious intolerance. Pogroms – ethnic massacres – were common. Any wild rumour or blatant lie was an acceptable excuse to seize Jewish property, torture, murder and evict innocent Jews, while the Church looked on approvingly.

The sensational details of the Lincoln murder were soon adapted into a variety of folk tales and ballads in which the anti-Jewish element gradually disappeared. Parents through the ages must have found this story useful for impressing on their children: "Never take sweets from a stranger".

"A Prince Who Speaks No Word of English"

1284

When English money shall become round
Then the Prince of Wales shall be crowned in London.

Thus ran the ancient prophecy of the bard Merlin. So when King Edward I issued new coins worth a halfpenny and a farthing, the Welsh stirred like a field of daffodils in a rising wind. Their leader, the mighty Llewellyn, led an insurrection against the newly-crowned King of England. Wild Welsh mountain men raided the western counties of England, and the bards swore to conquer London.

Edward had spent time in Wales and knew the terrain. He imported mountaineers from the Pyrenees, expert in mountain warfare. He armed a thousand pioneers with hatchets to hack their way through Welsh defences, and sent a fleet to attack Anglesey. To his dismay, Prince Llewellyn found himself alone and hunted.

To baffle his pursuers, he had a blacksmith re-shoe his horse with the horseshoes back-to-front, so as to leave misleading hoofprints. But the blacksmith ran squealing to the English, and they were soon on his trail again.

Crossing the River Wye, Llewellyn set the bridge alight behind him, leaving the English milling helplessly about on the opposite bank, unable to cross. But they simply trekked downstream until they found a place shallow enough to ford.

Still, Llewellyn did not have far to go to join the Welsh forces massing nearby, and lead them into one last, decisive battle. So hiding in a barn, he waited for his pursuers to give up and return to prepare for the battle. When everything fell silent, he ran outside, only to come face-to-face with a single rider, lance levelled . . .

Adam de Frankton wiped the tip of his lance on the grass and rode on to join his regiment. The battle went against the Welsh, who seemed confused and disorganized: only afterwards did the English discover why. Frankton rode back to the farmyard where he had stuck the running Welshman like a boar and left him bleeding to death. He found the man dead but, discovering the signet ring on his finger and the letters in his pocket, realized he had killed Prince Llewellyn! The Welsh had fought without a leader. It was no wonder they had lost.

"How does the prophecy go?" said Edward toying with the bloodstained letters which Frankton had brought him. "'Then shall the Prince of Wales be crowned in London?' Well, then. Cut off Llewellyn's head and carry it to London. Impale it on the walls of the Tower – and crown it as befits a traitor."

What did those blood-soaked letters recovered from Llewellyn's body say? Would they tell him which chieftains were loyal and which were not? With calm deliberation, Edward tossed the letters unopened into the fireplace and watched them burn. "They would only make me suspicious of men I would rather trust," he said.

It took more than one battle to subdue Wales. While Llewellyn's head, crowned with a wreath of ivy, glared out across London, Edward spent months in Wales, building fortresses, holding talks with surly chieftains. His wife Eleanor, to be close by her husband, lived first at Rhuddlan, then at newly completed Caernarvon Castle.

One day in April 1284, Edward was again in conference with Welsh chieftains – some restive and resentful, some resigned to defeat, some undecided what to make of this conciliatory Englishman who beat them in battle but still wanted their friendship. Today the King's thoughts were plainly elsewhere. When a messenger arrived, Edward pushed back his chair and hurried from the room.

He returned grinning, his face flushed with pleasure and with an announcement to make: "Meet me in one week at Caernarvon, my lords," he said, "and I will present you with a prince born in Wales who can speak no word of English nor ever did any wrong to man, woman or child!"

The Welsh were taken aback – delighted. What could it mean? A Welsh-speaking prince? The conference broke up excitedly and in a new mood of optimism.

It was a hushed, expectant gathering of shaggy, battle-scarred, weather-beaten, warriors, wrapped in Welsh-wool cloaks who crowded into the courtyard of Caernarvon Castle in the May sunshine to meet their new prince. Edward emerged to meet them, his queen at his shoulder. Cradled in his arms was a new-born baby. "According to my promise, I give you a prince born in Wales, who can speak no word of English!" and he lifted the baby high, for everyone to see.

The Welsh might have taken it for an insult – a joke at their expense. They did not. Edward was not deriding them. The baby Prince Edward was to have a Welsh nurse and Welsh servants, guaranteeing that his first words would be Welsh. Wales was no longer an independent country; it was a mere principality within Edward's kingdom. But conquerors have treated their vanquished foe far worse. One by one, the warlords came forward and, taking the baby's tiny hand between huge, gnarled fingers, kissing it through bushy beards, they swore an oath of loyalty to the English King.

A year later, Edward's first-born son, Alfonso, died, and the infant Edward became heir to the throne. At twenty-four he was crowned in Westminster Abbey.

So what of Merlin's prophecy?

When English money shall become round
Then the Prince of Wales shall be crowned in
London.

Until Edward I's "prophetic" issue of half-penny and farthing coins, the practice had been to cut pennies into halves and quarters. This encouraged the crime of "clipping" whereby people shaved slivers of silver off every piece of money which came their way. Introducing small-denomination coins and so doing away with the excuse to cut coins was one of Edward's first acts of reform in a long, intelligent reign.

The baby's mother, Queen Eleanor of Castile, bore Edward eleven children and shared his work for thirty-six years; the couple were devoted to each other. When she died in Nottinghamshire, Edward transported her body back to London, raising a stone cross wherever her body rested on the journey. Three of these nine Eleanor crosses still exist.

Unfortunately, the "Welsh-speaking" Prince Edward, in whose birth everyone took such delight, proved a grave disappointment as King Edward II. Forced to abdicate, he died in prison, probably murdered.

Robert the Bruce
and the Spider
1306-1314

"Robert the Bruce, lost, stolen or strayed!" read the English proclamation jeeringly, for the so-called King of Scotland had been gone all year and those trying to hunt him down could find no trace.

Dispossessed of his country by the English and driven to live as an outlaw, he and his companions were on the run, propping up branches for shelter, sleeping on animal skins, eating rabbits, berries and fish. With winter coming on, Robert the Bruce deemed it better the ladies should go to Kildrummie Castle, into the care of his young brother Nigel, while he and his few companions headed further north.

The news that reached them was all bad. Though Bruce kept his comrades entertained with stories of questing knights and poems about the heroes of Scotland, his spirits sank lower and lower. Every day, relations and friends were being captured, imprisoned, put to death. Perhaps he should abandon any dreams of driving the English out of Scotland. Six battles he had fought with the enemy, and six times his fortunes had fallen still lower.

One night, sheltering in a dilapidated hut on the island of Rathlin, he lay looking up at the roof. A

spider hung there from a single thread, trying to swing from one rafter to the next so as to establish a web. Again and again it tried, though surely the distance was too great. Four, five, six times it tried. What perseverance! Did it never know when to give up? Why did it not scuttle away into a corner and weave there? Bruce found himself oddly caught up in the efforts of the spider. His eyes hurt with watching it so intently. I too, have made six attempts, he thought. If this creature tries again – if it succeeds – then, by all that's holy *so will I*!

The little gossamer thread was barely visible, and yet from it now hung the rest of Bruce's life. He forgot to swallow. He forgot to blink. The spider gathered its legs into a single black pellet. Swinging across the dark chasm of the roof, the little trapeze artist reached its goal and began, without respite, to construct a gossamer kingdom between the rafters.

In that moment, a surge of determination swept through Robert the Bruce which drove out all his weariness and despair. He would live to see the English driven out, and to be acknowledged King of Scotland! "And when I do, I shall make a pilgrimage to Jerusalem to give thanks. This I swear, Lord!"

The spider brought no sudden change in Bruce's luck. He learned that Kildrummie Castle had been taken, and the ladies there – his sister and wife – had been shut up like wild beasts in wooden cages, and hung over the battlements. Another sister had been placed in a nunnery. And his young brother Nigel – no more than a boy – had been hanged. But now, instead of increasing his despair, such news only fuelled Bruce's zeal for revenge. Even though the people were too terrified to answer his call to arms, and two more of his brothers were captured and hanged, Robert the Bruce would not give up hope.

He gained the friendship of Black Douglas, terror of the Borders, and at last highland and lowland lairds began rallying to his cause. More and more castles were captured by his growing army.

At Stirling, King Edward sent against him the greatest army ever led by an English king. When it came into sight, Black Douglas reported back to Bruce that it was the "most beautiful and most terrible sight". Sixty thousand men, better mounted and better armed than the Scots, came on like cloud shadow over the landscape.

Bruce said, "If any man of you is not ready for either victory or death, let him leave now!" But not one man quit the field. The odds were against them two to one, but everyone knew that on this battle the future of Scotland rested: its independence, its nationhood, its pride. The lines were drawn up for the battle called Bannockburn.

"They are kneeling to beg forgiveness!" cried King Edward, thinking the Scots were going down on their knees in hope of mercy.

"Yes, but they are asking it from God, not from us," said an English baron. "They are praying. These men will conquer or die."

The English cavalry moved off, formidable in their fine armour, on their huge horses, speeding from a walk to a trot, from a trot to a canter. Helmet crests and pennons flickered as if a grass fire were devouring the plain . . . And then all of a sudden they were stumbling and pitching, their horses tripping and going down.

Knights fell from their ornate saddles and lay pinned to the ground by their weight of armour. Bruce had had his men dig 10,000 holes to the depth of a man's knee – 10,000 artificial rabbit holes in which a galloping horse could step and break a leg. Many of the horses and many of the knights did not stir, for Bruce had also strewn the plain with spiky calthrops which lie always with one lethal point upward.

Bruce's cavalry rushed the English archers: after that the English military advantage had gone. King Edward fled. The attendant who escorted him safely off the field (valuing his honour more than Edward did) turned back and threw himself into the mêlée to die fighting. But as the royal banner retreated, so the English ranks broke and ran, all the heart gone out of them.

The battle of Bannockburn established Robert the Bruce as King of Scotland. But the Pope said he would only acknowledge Bruce if he went on Crusade to the Holy Land.

No penance could have pleased Bruce more, remembering the vow he had made on Rathlin. He longed to see Jerusalem. But illness had dogged him down the years, and now it caught up with him. Leprosy prevented Bruce from keeping his promise to the Pope. So he sent for his best friend and bravest fighter, Black Douglas, and asked him, "Keep my promise. When I am dead, go to the Holy Land in my place. Carry my heart with you, and bury it in the Holy Sepulchre where Christ lay down and rose again to life."

Black Douglas did as he was asked. Though Robert the Bruce was buried, wrapped in cloth-of-gold, in Dunfermline Abbey, his heart, sealed in a lead casket, was worn around Douglas's neck the day he joined battle with the Infidel.

He had travelled only as far as Spain (then occupied by Moorish Moslems). Cut off from his troops, Douglas saw no escape. So he wrenched the casket from round his neck and hurled it forward, over-arm, crying, "Pass onward . . . ! I follow or die!"

The descendants of Douglas emblazon their shields with a bleeding heart surmounted by a golden crown to commemorate this last great act of loyalty and devotion.

King Edward II took with him to Scotland a Carmelite priest called Baston, renowned for his skill as a poet. The intention was that Baston should record in verse the King's glorious victory over the Scots. In the event, Baston was taken prisoner, and Robert the Bruce persuaded him to celebrate the Scottish triumph instead. His poem still exists.

After the battle of Bannockburn, the "wild men" of Scotland grew more and more audacious, annually raiding Durham and Northumbria. Peace was only struck when Bruce's young son, David, became betrothed to an English princess.

The Brawling Scottish Wench

1338

With a usurper on the throne of Scotland, hammered in place by English armies, the Scottish people seethed with indignation and resentment. Their loyalty was to the child king, David II, and despite a catastrophic defeat at Halidon Hill, when 10,000 Scots fell under a sleet of English arrows, individual strongholds still held out against the English invaders.

Away on the coast, its feet in the ocean, its face turned to the land, Dunbar Castle came under siege by the English. The lord of the castle was away, fighting in the cause of the young King David, leaving his wife in sole charge. But his wife was more formidable than many a knight; his wife was Agnes, daughter of Randolph. With her swarthy skin and the hairband worn low across her eyebrows, she had the look of a war stallion champing at the bit. And they called her Black Agnes.

William Montacute, Earl of Salisbury, pitched camp so as to isolate Dunbar on its rocky promontory. Then he brought up his great machines of war – his trebuchets. These gigantic catapults lobbed boulders in great arcs of destruction, demolishing whole sections of battlement, crumbling masonry like Scottish shortbread.

"Watch for the white flag," said Salisbury,

confidently expecting
Black Agnes to appear
pleading for her life.

And indeed,
shreds of fluttering
cloth did appear on
the battlements. A
group of women
moved slowly along
the parapet flicking
napkins. But not as flags

of surrender. They were *dusting* the castle walls,
flicking away grime and chippings, as though
Salisbury's trebuchets had simply spoiled their
housekeeping! Even some of the English troops gave a
gasping laugh of admiration at such cool audacity.

Salisbury was not amused. "*Bring up the sow!*" he
bellowed.

Now the "sow" was a siege engine with a sloping,
arrow-proof roof which enabled workmen to get close
up to a castle wall and work in safety, digging to
undermine the wall. The roof protected them from
archers on the battlements. Up trundled the sow now,
concealing dozens of English solders beneath its roof of
timber and hide.

Black Agnes peered over the wall.

"Beware, Montacute, your sow is about to have
piglets!" she called down.

Again a gasp from the English camp. For a gigantic
heap of debris – masonry, boulders from the beach and
sundry castle rubbish suddenly lurched forwards into
view, toppled from behind by crow bars. Tons of rock
cascaded over the battlements on to the sow below.

Agnes had predicted the exact spot at which Salisbury would attempt to break through. She had arranged the perfect answer to Montacute's sow. The hide roof smashed and splintered under the falling rock. The men beneath it screamed and went down, or ran for their lives squealing like demented piglets. "Oh look!" said Agnes, two hands clasped at her breast. "See the English piggies run!"

Earl Salisbury was spitting with rage.

Consequently, when a traitor came to his tent by night – a servant from the castle – the earl rubbed his hands with malicious delight. Now I have you, Black Agnes, he thought. "You say you can give the castle into my hands, man?"

"For gold enough," said the servant, "I can do King Edward that service. Come to the gate at midnight, and I'll tell you how."

With only his squire for company, William Montacute went at midnight – and, to his amazement, found the portcullis of Dunbar Castle raised just as high as a man's head! At this time of night, Agnes would be in her night-gown, sleeping. There was not even a sentry on watch! What could be easier? "Go on, go on in," he urged his squire.

With a rattle and a clank, the portcullis fell, its mesh of bars jarring the drawbridge on which Earl Salisbury was standing. On one side stood his squire, round-eyed with terror, fingers poking through the cullis, whimpering. On the other stood Salisbury. He had been within one pace of stepping into Agnes's trap, and though the trap had been sprung too early, he took to his heels now and ran, pursued all the way back to his tent by the ringing, rasping laughter of Black Agnes watching from the battlements.

Scottish minstrels were soon writing ballads about Black Agnes. One verse ran:

That brawling, boisterous, Scottish wench
Kept such a stir in tower and trench,
That came I early, came I late,
I found Black Agnes at the gate.

Relief arrived at Dunbar Castle from the seaward side, and the Earl of Salisbury was obliged to abandon his siege after nineteen humiliating weeks. David the Bruce, for whom Dunbar and Lochleven had loyally held out, later launched a foolhardy invasion of England while King Edward III was away fighting in France.

He underestimated Edward's wife, Queen Philippa (another formidable lady), who rallied four divisions of men and annihilated David's army in Northumberland. David, despite one arrow in his head and another in his nose, fought on for three hours until taken prisoner. He was transported south to the Tower of London, where his wife joined him . . . and while the misery in Scotland continued unabated, enjoyed a pleasant eleven years as part of the English court, attending banquets and tournaments and balls.

The Black Prince Wins His Spurs

1346

He was only sixteen, and barely able to contain his pride, as his father, the King, dubbed him a knight. For almost as long as Prince Edward could remember, England had been at war with France, but this was to be his first military expedition and the biggest of the war – a foray into northern France, with the chance of rich pickings.

Then, somehow the King overreached himself and suddenly he was in retreat, chased by the full might of French nobility and half of Europe with them. Sixteen-year-old Prince Edward did not regret the turn of events, but it looked as if his first campaign was going to end not quite according to plan.

King Philip of France and 68,000 men were marching to confront a mere 7,800 English and Welsh. But Prince Edward's worst fear was not of dying. It was of being sent away to a place of safety: heir to the throne, too precious to lose, too young to be trusted with his own life. To his great relief, it did not happen. Instead, his father invited him and the other knights and earls to dine in his tent on the eve of battle, and to offer up prayers. No mention was made of preserving his life.

The Prince determined to observe and learn. There would never be a bigger or better lesson in kingship and military command. So he watched everything. He saw how his father, armed with only a white wand, surveyed his troops, encouraging them, making jokes, telling them to eat well and take a glass of wine. He saw how the archers – the great bowmen of England – settled down to sleep under their blankets, in the teeming rain, helmets by their feet. He ran his unpractised eye over Crécy Hill, struggling to interpret his father's strategy.

He swelled with pride at being given command of 3,800 men; he bridled a little at being given the Earl of Warwick and Sir Godfrey de Harcourt to help command them. But he was glad enough of their wisdom and advice when, out of the morning rain, the French army came lumbering into view – a solid mass of armour and silks and saddleclothes, of bannerets, nodding horses and slogging footsoldiers, all bearing down on Crécy Hill.

His thoughts then were a wild confusion of prayers, fears and hopes, dense as the flock of ravens and crows which circled over the battlefield. And yet some part of his brain went on seeing with icy clarity.

He saw the French advancing – then the French heralds darting to and fro trying to tell them to halt: King Philip had not yet formed his battle plan. The army would not or could not halt: its numbers were too vast to absorb the command.

He saw the Genoese crossbowmen in the front – 1,800 of them – fumbling with their weapons in the downpour, the strings too wet to be strung. He noted, by contrast, the steely composure of the English bowmen as they rose to their feet, undaunted by their night on the muddy hill. From under their helmets they drew dry bowstrings, calmly and deliberately strung their longbows – and fired.

As in a dream, Edward saw that sleet of arrows, that whistling storm within a storm. For lightning was crackling between sky and earth and the air was smoky with rain. At noon the sun went out: darkness ate it away bit by bit: a dread omen for one side or the other. Then the Genoese were running from the storm of arrows, running and being hacked down by their own side for getting in the way, clogging up the road.

Now the French knights were within range of the arrows. Riderless horses capered and reared in terror, though those behind kept pushing forward, unaware of what was happening at the front. Forward went the Prince's Welshmen – the Cornishmen too – with their gruesome long knives – *snicker-snack!* – dealing out death in the midst of the milling confusion.

The clouds drew back to reveal the sun, restored after its eclipse, shining full in the face of the French, blinding them. *There* was the strategy of Crécy Hill! Prince Edward flushed full of hot pride in his father who rode now helmetless through the field.

One tiny scene of heroism fixed itself in the boy's mind: the old blind King of Bohemia riding into battle between two French knights, their bridles tied together so as to steer the old man's horse. Flank against flank they rode, Bohemia's white plumes nodding proudly as he rode to certain destruction, fighting the noisy darkness until it overwhelmed him. Edward rose in his saddle to see what became of the three . . .

Then suddenly, as if from nowhere, two French regiments were closing on his own flank. They had skirted round the chaos in mid-field to attack the Prince of Wales.

After that, Edward felt nothing except the hot churning hysteria of battle – lashing out, kill-or-be-killed. All those strokes and parries practised for tedious hours in the tilt yard came back to him now. But for every Frenchman he killed, two more seemed to materialize. Out of the corner of his eye, he saw the Earl of Warwick dispatch a herald to fetch help.

But help did not come. The King refused to send it. "Is my son dead, then? Or unhorsed, or so badly wounded that he cannot defend himself?"

"No, thank God, but he is in great need of your help!" panted the herald.

"Then go back to those who sent you and tell them not to send again nor expect me to come. Let my boy win his spurs, for I am determined that the glory and honour of this day shall be given to him!" Some who heard him asked themselves: what manner of man refuses help to his son?

The troops arrayed on Crécy Hill did not break rank, or chase after the French when the French scattered, or rush down to plunder the dead. Disciplined to the last, the bowmen stood longest, until night was resting on their bowtips, and hymns of thanksgiving were flocking into the darkening sky along with the ravens and crows. Bonfires were lit; an army of torches were lit from the bonfires.

Those who had seen the prince fight were full of admiration, calling him his father's son, dubbing him "the Black Prince". The King came looking for his son, his hood of mail pushed back. Those nearby said that there were tears in his eyes. "Sweet son," he said, rushing to embrace the boy, searching every inch of his face. "You are indeed my son, for you have acquitted yourself most loyally this day and you are worthy to be a king!"

"The victory was all yours, Father."

"Nay, yours, son, yours!" There was a wild relief in the King's face which hinted how hard it had been for him not to send help.

From the prince's hand drooped three ostrich feathers, specked with blood. He had recovered them from the helmet of the fallen King of Bohemia, along with the old man's device: "*Ich dien*". "I serve".

"It shall be my device now," he said, "and the coat of arms of every Prince of Wales to come."

Then the battle-fever drained out of him and he was left white-faced and weary, with trembling limbs: sixteen again, for all his glittering spurs.

The battle of Crécy was a legendary triumph arising out of supreme discipline on one side and horrendous bungling and over-confidence on the other. Reputedly, King Philip escaped with just five knights.

It occurred at the height of the Age of Chivalry, and the Black Prince is a highly chivalrous figure – brave, honourable, godly, courteous. Why the Black Prince? Not, apparently, because of the colour of his armour, but "styled black by terror of his arms", i.e. because he was so terrifying in battle.

The three feathers and motto "*Ich dien*" are still the device of the Prince of Wales, though the Welsh hotly maintain that the words are not Germanic but Welsh, meaning "A free servant".

"Oss! Oss!" "Wee Oss!"

1347

The French invaders came, thinking it would be easy to help themselves to the wealth of Padstow.

Across the Channel, Calais was under siege, and the fishermen and shopkeepers, the craftsmen and farmers of the little Cornish port had built two ships by their own efforts and set sail to help King Edward capture the city. No sooner were they gone than a fleet of French ships, knowing Padstow lay unprotected, sailed the other way, thinking to take over the town.

But they had not reckoned with Ursula Birdhood.

"Fetch out your red cloaks and your scarlet petticoats!" Ursula told the women of the town, "and meet me at Stepper Point!"

If Ursula was a witch, she was a wholesome witch, and if there was magic in her, it was of a very ancient kind. And her magic was small alongside that of the 'Obby 'Oss, dancer-in of the May!

Every May Day, from before daybreak till long after dark, the Padstow Hobbyhorse dances through the streets, twirling and leaping on its twin thin legs, its black cloth body flapping, its black conical body as pointed and jaunty as a witch's hat. And all the while it dances, it drives out winter and fetches in spring.

Now the French were invading, with swords sharp as winter and faces cruel as February, and nothing but a handful of women to keep them out. By the time Ursula Birdhood and the women of Padstow reached the headland at Stepper Point, a crescent of French warships was dropping anchor in the bay.

If those women were frightened, they sang the fear out of their throats. If their legs were shaking, they danced the fright out of their legs. In a deep, gruff voice, Ursula Birdhood began to sing and everyone joined in the familiar words:

"Unite and unite and let us unite
For summer is acome unto day . . ."

A drum took up the beat – a jogging, syncopated beat, like a horse trotting over broken ground:

"And whither we are going we will all unite
In the merry morning of May!"

They sang the Night Song and after that the Day Song, even richer with magic:

"O where is St George
O where is he O?
He is out in his long-boat all on the salt sea O.
Up flies the kite and down falls the lark O . . ."

Out at sea, the Frenchies saw the flicker of red cloth on the top of Stepper Point, though the singing was too far off to be heard.

"Il y a quelqu'un!"
"La! En haut!"
"Les soldats anglais?"

They pointed, shouting.

Then, indistinct among the red glimmer of moving figures, they saw another shape – one which struck far more fear into their superstitious souls: a big flapping creature, black and headless, conical as a witch's hat and madly leaping on tireless legs – a creature they could make no sense of, unless . . . unless it was . . .

"Le Diable! Le Diable hors d'Infer!"

Had the English won the Devil over to their side, and were they even now whipping up magic on Stepper Point headland to sink the French, to crack their hulls like eggshells, to whisk their souls away like spray off the white wave tops? From time to time a single unheard voice exhorted, "Oss! Oss!" – but the dancers shouted their answer loud enough for the cry to cross the water: "Wee Oss!"

The French weighed anchor and sailed away. Ursula Birdhood watched them go, standing on the headland, red cloak streaming out behind her, one hand knotted in the tail of the nodding, skittering Hobbyhorse of Padstow.

This same story – of dancing women in red scaring off a French invasion – is told in at least one other place, across the Severn Estuary, in Wales. So it is unlikely both versions are true, but all the more likely that something of the sort did happen *somewhere*.

Age-old songs can become altered over the years into gobbledegook. One Padstow verse which runs:

'Aunt Ursula Birdhood she had an old ewe
And she died in her own Park O'

But until 1850 the 'Obby 'Oss dancer was accompanied through the streets of Padstow on May Day by a character representing "an old woman in a red cloak". Was she Aunt Ursula? The horse itself has its origins in a Celtic religion older than Christianity, and brings fertility and renewal. It used to be thought that if the 'Oss threw its skirts over a young wife, she would give birth within the year.

The Padstow celebration is one of the most exciting and genuine folk rituals still observed in England. Most were suppressed or "adopted" by Christianity, or frozen out by disapproving Victorians.